c

Raised by Gypsies,
Surrounded by Dreamers,
Rooted A Rebel

c. michelle bryant griffin

c. michelle bryant griffin

Dedicated to the late

erik scott anderson

The legacy of your beautiful soul remains an impression in my heart and life forever. Not a day goes by that you are not missed, mentioned, or running through my mind.

raised by gypsies, surrounded by dreamers, rooted a rebel

table of contents

c. michelle bryant griffin

chapter one

The Ripple of One

At the writing of this book, I am a spry, 55 years, healthy, free-spirited young woman. I say young because, despite what my creaky knees, weak bladder, arthritic hands, and poor vision tell me, for the most part, I FEEL young. Mostly because it was in my fifties I came to discover, know, experience and like my true self. I feel I have led a rich, full life and my days, my mission and my purpose are just beginning. It took me reaching my 50's to find happiness outside of another person and to be ok with me. I wish I had been more like this when I was younger. There is no telling what I could have accomplished and the ripple effect I might have left.

In addition to being a self-published author of five books, I am an entrepreneur, artist, speaker, and a published, multi-award-winning photographer. I have shared my talent, story, passion, and light through various engagements across the United States from Florida to Alaska and appeared on several local, city and nationally syndicated radio stations. In addition, I was blessed to have ministered to over two dozen youth at a residential treatment facility for boys and girls under the age of eighteen who were suffering from emotional issues such as abuse and neglect. I feel I have shined my light and I speak from the heart in an encouraging, inspiring and transparent manner about my childhood, adolescence of abuse, and a marriage of struggle. I offer a gift of hope, healing and a message of victory and empowerment to those who feel they are alone in their own personal wars.

I have been writing since I could pick up a pencil, and it often served as a form of therapy for me. In fact, for the most part, many of my diary entries were only submitted during the tumultuous times in my life. Looking back, I recognize much of my creativity has been derived from emotional experiences and the traumas, obstacles and heartaches I endured.

It is only now that I delve deep and reflect on the people I have known in various ways and degrees. I recall the good ones, bad ones, the ugly and mean ones, the wise, the goofs and the ones who always marched to a different drum. The impressions deposited on my life and heart vary and yet stand out in monumental ways. And it occurs to me there are 720 minutes in a day when we may knowingly or unintentionally be impacting or depositing into someone emotionally, whether it is your children and their friends, to the grumpy neighbor, to the checkout girl at the grocery store, or to your server at lunch. It could be someone we may or may not even know. Let me ask you this: given any situation, if you knew that moment was the last moment you would have on this earth, with that person or people, what would you do differently?

In the next few chapters, I hope to tackle and reflect on the effects we have on people and how they impact us, the deposits that are made into who we eventually become and the ripple effect that typically occurs, often without even realizing. It is my desire once you have finished this book and close the back cover, you will have examined why you are who you are and why you react the way you respond. I am confident I have not recognized every single person who impacted or influenced me in one way or another, as my memory is not what it used to be. However, I have highlighted those who stand out the most to me in numerous ways and by various means. Hopefully, as you travel with me through times in my life, you will gain insight as to who you want to represent yourself as and how you may be impacting those you encounter every minute you are on this earth from the beginning of your life to the end.

chapter two

Baby Steps

L et's begin, well, at the beginning. It is a glorious day! Mom is doing fine. Dad is super excited, and the baby is happy, healthy and home. By most accounts, when a baby is born, it is brought into a loving, caring, safe and warm environment. I know that was the case with my first child. When we brought him home from the hospital, we laid him on the bed and stared at him in endless wonder. Despite our best efforts, there was no way to comprehend what beautiful marvel was lain before us, let alone grasp the plethora of our feelings. We had created this, and now we were responsible for a human life. It was no different with my second or with any of my grandchildren. As with most new babies, we melted with every smile, gasped with every wail, and cried with every tear. Almost immediately, babies unknowingly embed themselves within our hearts from the minute they arrive. I cannot think of another time in our lives when a single person has that much involuntary control or impact over our hearts and emotions, let alone encompasses so much of our being, like that of an infant.

It is even in the most horrendous, poignant cases of an infant abandoned, neglected, abused, mistreated, or tossed aside there is such an enormous impact made on the lives and hearts of those made aware. I find it remarkable, without even realizing it from the moment we enter this world, we are making an impression on someone. Our purpose, our assignment or mission on this earth is already beginning.

From infancy, we have people wrapped around our fingers, catering to our every impetuous whim. We have all our desires frequently met. Quickly, we realize when we cry we get picked up, fed, or cleaned. We are often rocked, snuggled, cuddled, or held close, rarely leaving someone's side, hip, shoulder, or chest. As we get a bit older, we learn the words NO and MINE and hopefully, please and thank you. We understand what others mean to us. People bigger and older begin to make decisions for us, influence us in our behavior, our actions, and our dispositions. Even on a small scale, we discover the difference between right and wrong, along with the repercussions, rewards, and consequences for the choices and actions we choose. We thoroughly watch, observe, and mock those around us, imitating traits and characteristics both good and bad. Have you ever had a three-year call you an asshole because he heard his mother say that to her husband? I have. It seemed both humorous and appalling to me at the same time, yet it is something I still remember it to this day and was an action deposited into my memory bank.

Even as grown adults, my children have impacted me. I have learned so much from raising them, watching them, sharing life experiences with them. I consider myself blessed to have been able to introduce manners, ethics, and traditions that they now pass on to their children and implement in their own adult lives.

My youngest grandson is two at this writing and is in the imitating stage of his growth. His mother tells me of a story of when while driving, she abruptly put on the brakes to avoid a collision only to hear "oh shit!" come from the little car seat behind her. It is easy to see how that moment made an impression on both that day. I am reminded of a country song called "Watching You" by Rodney Adkins with similar lyrics. Without realizing, we influence others by our actions and words. Fortunately, my daughter was able to curb those actions in future situations and be more aware of the influences she makes in her son's development.

4

Unfortunately, it is often many circumstances in life we are not so privileged. Many times it is anger, emotions, jealousy, or stresses of life that trigger reactions and cause us ultimately to infect someone negatively rather than impact them on a positive level. I have come to the point in my life where I despise drama (especially unwarranted drama). I make a conscious choice to pick what will stress me out, avoid parts of my life (people and situations) that cause me undue stress or drama, clinging to peace, contentment, and problem-solving for a better way of life. It indeed is possible if one is willing to put in the effort at each encounter.

chapter three

Infect or Impact?

There are many ways we can be impacted or influenced by another individual. In this chapter, we will visit numerous ways, means, and people with some connective influences and various moments in my own life to shed light on this point. As discussed previously, we are making an impression on someone in our life from the moment we are born. Perhaps from the moment of the knowledge of life within us. Think about it, when you found out you were going to be a parent, your life changed at that very moment, and the child had not yet entered the world. I find that to be colossal.

From early childhood to adolescence, we encounter many stimuli — parents, teachers, pastors, and other relatives to name a few. Our mother is probably the first person we recall impacting us. My mother was a very young mother when she gave birth to me while still in high school. I remember stories of being very attached and clingy to her in my early young years. I suppose, as with most children, in my primary years, I looked to her as my protector, my comfort, and my security. I'm sure I knew without a doubt, that when I was with her everything would be all right and she would take care of all my needs. It was unspoken. Throughout my teen years, I remember her as a devoted wife and mother, who always spoke her mind and never sugar coated anything she said to me. One always knew where they stood with her - good or bad. She always seemed to give 100% to anything she did, strove for perfection, and refused to settle for mediocrity or imitation.

We have always had a tumultuous relationship, my mother and me; perhaps it is because we are so much alike. But I can say she is my best friend and I do not know where my life would be without her. My mother always encouraged me to be an original and not to be like anyone else. Today, I am blessed that my mother is alive and is an active part of my daily life. Although miles away, I call on her for advice, insight, critique, and opinion because I know she will always be forthright in her responses. My mother has instilled many values in me I carry on to this day and often find myself saying, "My mother always said." Or I catch myself doing something or acting a certain way, especially when I was raising my children, I would think to myself, "I've become my mother." THAT is not a bad thing as I have great respect and admiration for my mother and often she remains the calm in my storm, my security and comfort, even if she is merely a voice on the other end of the telephone.

As a child or even as an adult, I believe we tend to put our parents, especially our mothers, in a box. They are our Mom, period. Irreplaceable. We tend to disregard the fact they are real people and have feelings, emotions, and may even be enduring their own personal battles and demons while continuing their role. These are things I know I never saw in my mother until the notion and my memory collided when I became the age she was at that time. This reminiscence caused me to wonder how I would handle a specific situation she endured. It is those moments I have an even more profound respect for my mother.

For example, it has been nearly forty years, but I recently reconnected and spoke with a childhood friend. In part of our conversation, he asked, "How is your mother? She was always so kind to me. I remember when my mother died, my first phone call was to you. I was talking to you on the phone, and your mom took the phone and said, 'Oh honey, I am so sorry to hear about your mom. Just know that we love you and if you need anything we are here for you.'" As I explained to my friend that mom was doing well, my heart swelled with pride. Today, as an adult, I am aware of much of what my mother went through during that time in our lives forty years ago. Despite an abusive, controlling marriage, working outside the home endless hours to make ends meet, and putting up the "everything is fine" front to her peers, in the heart of my childhood friend forty years later, my mom's words and actions in that one moment are still embedded. She merely was her genuine self, no motives, no ultimatums, no selfish acts. Just a loving person with a caring heart and a kind mother to a hurting teenager. What an impact that single action made.

My fathers (yes, plural) on the other hand were a different story. There's more to the story but simply put, my biological father left my mother, my brother, my sister and me when I was not even three to pursue his college dream. I did not reconnect with him until my late teens. At that point in my life, I felt I had grown up missing a loving father figure, deprived of being daddy's little girl and all that came with that title. For instance, I had not shared the kiss your boo-boos when you fall off your bike (or even learned how to ride for that matter) or experienced the "so you want to date my daughter" moments that I thought were standard in father/daughter relationships. I did not feel the protection and security that often are great accolades on Father's Day cards. Truth be told, Father's Day is difficult for me as I can never find a Father's Day card that fits my relationship with my biological father. He wasn't there to tell me I looked beautiful at any of my dances or proms or present at any of my award ceremonies, or school production opening night, etc. However, as it only seemed fitting, in my mid-twenties, I did ask him to walk me down the aisle at my wedding, and he did. Although we do keep in touch, our relationship has never been very close, despite our best efforts. The only common ground we tend to share is our children. My son is only a few years younger than his two sons by his second wife. I stretch to think of a time he has impacted or influenced me in any way. Most of his words have been harsh, and if I am not of the same opinion as he, it just brings confrontation to our conversations. Perhaps it is his age, and he is set in his ways. Maybe I am young, a Pollyanna (as he likes to refer to me) or perhaps I am simple minded. To me, he does not seem to listen if the topic is not of interest or benefit him. Often it seems he finds minor things a nuisance and annoying; he lacks patience even when it comes to ordering at a restaurant. I often feel he places me beneath my other siblings, although I am his firstborn. Repeatedly, I am reminded of the story of when he sold his prized 1957 Thunderbird convertible to pay for my birth and fifty-five years later he still chuckles and says, "It was not a fair trade."

I searched for him as soon as I turned sixteen. When I first met him, he showed me a worn-out, faded photo of my brother, sister, and me in his wallet. It had been there so long; it was stuck to the plastic sleeve. Seeing it made me feel loved, wanted, missed, and special. I recall early in our relationship talking on the phone, as I lived many cities away. I phoned him at his office one day, and as a shy, confused sixteen-year-old girl trying to rekindle and build a new (though awkward) relationship with her father, I timidly asked if I could call him daddy. At first, he did not answer. It was only after a brief silence he said, "I'm sorry I had to shut the door." Through the sniffling on the other end of the line, I could tell he was crying. I felt that effect through all the miles and still remember its impression on me to this day.

I have to confess that despite the disconnect between my father and I, when thinking about my him, I am taken to a very horrific moment for me in my late forties. At the time, I lived in southeast Georgia and he lived in southern Florida. Although he visited my other siblings who lived within an hour from me, he never visited me, saw my apartment, or showed any interest in my single life after divorce. Now mind you, I had been through many tragic moments in my life, but this particular one nearly destroyed me. Many have no idea although I tried to outline and gain healing through the writing of my third book, In an Instant. It was during that horrendous time in my life that my father showed up without warning, took me to lunch, lent a kind ear, offered advice, and just sat in the restaurant booth with his big burly arms around me. I never felt so safe as at that moment; I honestly felt at that moment like I had a Dad. I would like to say my father and I have a good relationship. Truthfully, I believe it's cordial at best. I doubt I will ever live up to his expectations of me. All that aside, I am grateful I found him and that he is in my life. He has, perhaps unknowingly, left some positive deposits on who I am. Earlier, in fact, up until a few years ago, I devoted myself to seeking his approval and making him proud of the person I had become. Now, I am content to be me and am okay admitting if something doesn't meet his approval, then it's still okay. As my mother always taught me, it's better to be the best YOU that you can be than 1,000 copies of someone else. I'm okay with me. He's entitled to his opinion. I once heard "You can be the ripest, juiciest, peach in the world and there will still be somebody who doesn't like peaches." Painfully, when it's your parent, it stings a bit. But after all these years, I've come to grips with it and accept it.

Here is a poem I wrote for him for Father's Day when I was in my twenties. I spelled daddy differently because our relationship was unlike most father/daughter relationships.
dadi-

did you ever think of mi?
i used to wonder when i was small,
if you ever cried or ever cared
and why you never called.

so much of mi was empty,
so much of mi was lost,
so i set my sights on finding you,
no matter what the cost.

though scared and unaware
of just what i might find,
i still needed to tell my dadi,
that he'd never left my mind.

well the day arrived and then we met,
and i very nearly cried.
for walking right there with mi
was my dadi by my side.

so much pride filled the holes,
that haunted mi so long,
and once i found my dadi
nothing could go wrong.

so dadi here's to you
for being the man you are,
for being my dadi these past few years
even though we were apart.

though today i might be so much different
if i'd had you all along,
i know that since i've found you,
nothing can go wrong.

happy father's day!

~~~

Regrettably, the only father I knew from age three to sixteen, was my step-father and to say he was not a nice person would be too gracious for someone of his merit. He was physically, emotionally, and sexually abusive, manipulative, and aggressive. I was a continual pawn in a cruel game of passive-aggressive I hate you - you're worthless, I love you - you're special, throughout all my formative years. It is because of his face, within inches of mine screaming obscenities and shouting cruel, harsh words as his finger shook and spit splattered, that I still react when anyone shakes a finger in my face even in jest or storytelling. Now, I'm not one to blame others for our mistakes or shortcomings or play the victim card, but I openly accredit my lack of self-worth and uncertainty of my capabilities, talents, and offerings to the words and actions embedded in me to his negative impact in my life. Einstein said, "Everyone is born a   genius. But if you judge a fish on his ability to climb a tree, it will live its whole life believing it is stupid." That was the underlying message of much of my life. Truth is, I WAS born a genius but it seemed I was never smart enough, pretty enough, creative enough, or good enough to please my stepfather, no matter the efforts I attempted. I did not realize at that young age I still had choices; I did not have to allow him to have that kind of control or effect on me. The things we learn in hindsight.

My senior year of high school was riotous. I wanted desperately to escape my home life but felt the weight of leaving young siblings behind to be devoured in the secret prison I had known. I tried the "if I say something nice, he'll think differently" approach and wrote him a poem. I stood with shaking knees as I recited it to him. Here is that poem:

oh, daddy, you've loved mi through it all
you've helped mi as i grew,
you've made mi someone with pride and strength
i've always looked up to you.

you carried mi off as a child,
a stranger you brought mi up real well,
now i'm someone with pride and strength
i'm someone they call michelle.

i know we've had our mishaps
times when life's not swell.
i've gained a lot of pride and strength
and i've become michelle.
 oh, daddy, i can't believe it
at times i was so vile,
you gave mi all my pride and strength
you held mi close awhile.

because of you, i am what i am
because of you, i live
you put up with my faults and weaknesses
gave all you had to give.

because of you, i am someone
because of you, i've grown
now, i've got my pride and strength
i can make it on my own.

oh daddy, thank you seems so little
i love you, even less
all i can think of daddy,
is i think you're the best.

~~~

After reading it to him, I walked over, handed it to him and kissed him on the cheek. Taking it from my hand and rising from his seated position, without saying a word, he walked over to the trash can, crumpled the paper and threw it away.

I was a very skinny and homely child and teenager. I recall a family picnic when my stepfather asked my sister to get him a toothpick. Playing with my other siblings, my sister came and said, daddy wants you. When I went to him and said, sir? He asked what I wanted. I said, "Sandy told me you wanted me." He busted out laughing. I hate to think THAT incident had such an impact, that there is some deep-set root causing my weight issues to this day, but the impression is still active and naturally embedded. A few months before graduation, I received a scholarship to a college and made my mind up to accept the offer and move forward with my life. Upon leaving, I left him this poem.

i tried to tell you
but you refused to understand.
i needed you to hug mi
but you wouldn't even touch my hand.

 i'm leaving home
yep, i'm on my way.
there's nothing you can do
to persuade mi to stay.

you're the one who's run mi off,
the one who didn't seem to care.
you're the reason i'm leaving
maybe i'll call you when i'm there.

you always needed to be right
and told mi i was wrong.
you didn't like the way i did things
yet, i tried to act more strong.

i tried not to let you get to mi
i tried to clear you from my head

but it's no use, you always drive mi to the ground
i hear you yelling when i'm in bed.

but it's all over now
there's nothing you can do.
i tried my hardest
and still can't put up with you.

sometimes you've been okay
and sometimes even fun,
but each little gripe and complaint
has turned into just one.

maybe you'll look back someday,
see yourself in my place.
i just can't take it anymore
i'm exhausted from the pace.

there's nothing you can say
sorry just won't get it.
if you think you can make mi stay
you might as well forget it.

~~~

As you can see, the influences of these two father figures left
emotional marks and impacts that remain with me to this day.
Ultimately, it was insecurity that led me in my twenties, to seek
someone who would spoil me and treat me like royalty, yet into a
toxic marriage that ultimately was destined for failure before it
began. As well as, endless menial jobs, a life of self-loathing and
self-searching and a lot of wasted talent that could have blossomed
so much sooner.

Perhaps it was that wounded reed of a person I had grown to
become, who was attracted to another wounded reed when I met
Jim. In my mid-twenties, I relocated to a different town to change
my life and begin anew. When I met Jim, I was independent, self-
sufficient and found him rather childish and annoying. He was
failing college, partied too much and worked part-time at a local

pizza place. His life ambition at the time was to be a state trooper. He lived with his mother and younger brother. Over time we were often caught sharing abusive step-father stories. Jim had lots of stories of how his step-father used him as a punching bag for most of his formative years. He told me of the name-calling and ridicule. I could see how these words and actions left an impression on him. In addition to feeling a kindred connection with Jim, I craved the he willingly showed me. Jim thought I hung the moon and was ever persistent to get my attention at any cost, even though he told me he felt I was out of his league. I had never been made to feel so special by anyone of the opposite sex who didn't want something in return. In time, persistence paid off and Jim and I married. His self-esteem was still shattered even into his adult years, to the point his confidence suffered tremendously. Our marriage of nearly 25 years was tumultuous at best. Through those years, Jim and I experienced many career changes, lost a child, experienced religious differences and were both weighed down with baggage. Despite what we carried into marriage with us, we also had two children, an amazing military career that led him to pursue and receive several Military awards and accolades and multiple college degrees. Jim and I grew to become better people because of knowing each other but amicably divorced in 2009. Our relationship has remained one of friendship and respect. Though we still don't see eye to eye on many things and after five minutes, drive each other crazy, nearly ten years later, we still can come together and be not only civil and cordial but compassionate and kind toward one another.

It would be difficult to spend nearly 30 years with someone and they not leave an impact on you. Although there are negative and positive musings in my relationship with Jim, the overall impact has been good, and I consider my life blessed having known him and sharing the majority of my life with him. Jim is a good person, has an amazing heart and as a medical professional, a bedside manner second to none. We are merely two people, who despite best efforts, bring out the worst in each other instead of the best. But since our divorce, we have come together, even with significant others beside us and joined in our children's weddings, moves, graduations, family funerals and reunions. My family members still consider him part of our family. They do so in part because of the type of man he is, the way he has treated me through the years and because of the impact he has left on them.

Speaking of family influences, my mother remarried late in her 40s, a man she met through a classified ad. She lived in Arizona at the time and he in Alaska. Seeing a segment on Oprah about there being 20 Alaska men to one woman, my then-divorced mother took out an ad in the personals of a local Alaska newspaper. With over 70 responses, she particularly liked the note and picture of the man relaxing on a rock with his floppy hat and fishing pole. Pen pals first for quite a while, she eventually, packed up her old car, daughter, and grandson and prayed they made it to Alaska safely. In my book, Papa was the cream of the crop where men are concerned. He had four daughters that lived all over of which I have friendly relationships. He was married to my mother for over 25 years and absolutely adored her. Every day his heart and soul simply glowed when he spoke of her or was near her. The women in my family are independent, strong, stubborn, and self-sufficient and it takes a special man to love us. Papa fit the bill perfectly.

Papa was a veteran, photographer, and outdoorsman with creative talent in woodworking making amazing lamps, sculptures, furniture and more. He loved coffee brandy and good conversation around a campfire. He attracted people wherever he was. But mostly, Papa believed in me. He believed in my abilities and always had an encouraging word to say to me. He died several years ago, and left a hole in all our hearts, but the impact he created on our lives runs deep.

chapter four

The Impression of an Honorable Knight

If you read my first book, God, are You listening? then you are familiar with Erik, my shining knight at the impressionable young age of fifteen. This particular book is dedicated to him. It pains me that on this day, as I write this actual chapter, I have learned of his untimely and unexpected death. He and his lovely wife of twenty-something years owned a silkscreen shop in south Florida. She ran the front, and he did the printing. From my understanding, they had lunch at the shop and she went to the back room to grab something. When she returned, Erik was slumped over on a piece of equipment. My only solace is knowing he died doing something he loved, in a place where he was able to be creative, and that he was with his wife. But today, my heart aches and so, as usual for me, I must write. How appropriate to work on a book about the impressions we leave on others when Erik left such a significant influence on me for the forty years I'd known him. As an awkward but kind-hearted, teenage young man, I credited Erik with saving me from a life of mental anguish. It is even after reconnecting thirty years later while dealing with my divorce when I saw myself as damaged goods that he reminded me I was much more and as he so eloquently put it, I should "be beautiful and let the world catch up." In many of our late-night online conversations, he   graciously gave words of wisdom to a hurting heart and bruised soul. It was through his eyes, I was able to see myself. His words, wisdom, and kindness have been permanently embedded within me and rooted deep in who I am today.

Erik was humble, gracious, and kind, as a boy and as a man. He was creative and loved an excellent Mead beer, unique music, art, and science fiction. Although often a Viking or renaissance among his peers, he was very grounded, simple, and down to earth. He seemed to have time to comfort anyone or extend an ear to those who needed one. He claimed I put him on too high a pedestal in my first book and had no idea the extent to which he had touched me and my life. He was and is truly a noble knight if ever one walked this earth, and his presence will be missed in my life and others I'm sure.

Often there is someone in our life, who is set apart from others, the ones who love us unconditionally, not our parents or family. They are the ones who believe in us when we doubt ourselves, motivate us when we feel our failures are encompassing our being, and don't tend to accept our pity parties as permanent solutions. I have been blessed to have had many in my life.

My current husband, Benny, is one of those people. He saw me when I was invisible, while I was searching for myself. Benny saw something in me, in my stubbornness, my drive to be independent at all costs, and believed in me from the beginning. He took a chance on me, made an investment in me, and eventually made me his wife. He is my rock and my sounding board, my business consultant and partner, but mostly my best friend. He tells it like it is and does not sugar coat anything. He sees things in a way that are different from my rose-colored glasses Pollyanna perspective and shows me various points of view. He promotes and endorses me personally and professionally in a way no one else does. He takes his vested interest beyond the typical. Benny has no tolerance for my pity parties or my "it's too hard" mumbo jumbo and therefore, refuses to allow me to linger there for long. He reminds me continually of my why and my purpose in my business and in my personal existence. Benny is the wind in my sails, a gift and a blessing in my life, and it is because of him I can share my gifts, talents, and passion with the world.

chapter five

Where We Left Off

Through my years, I have been blessed to have great like-minded friends who believed in me, who see something in me that I might not necessarily see in myself. During my seven-year stint in Alaska, I can honestly say I had the best support system I have ever had at any point in my life. My friends were REAL "Tell It Like It Is" friends who loved me unconditionally -- flaws, quirks and all. I had many who were there completely and without reproach, but a few stand out for me in influencing my life. For example, Taffy was creative and talented, everything she touched was beautiful from woodworking to scrapbooking. Our families went camping and fishing together during the summer. She and I shared crafting, mothering, and other fun things. She volunteered to watch my children during the summer, so I could work. She was also a great confidant and friend. I could tell her anything, and she received me with open arms, never judging. Although I have been out of Alaska for years now, Taffy and I are still friends and remain in touch online. She recently sent me a very long catching up letter along with a beautiful beaded necklace and earring set she hand made. I miss her much and hope to see her on a trip to Alaska someday.

Then there is Ruby. When I first met Ruby, I did not like her. She was brash, bold, and a bit harsh. And yes, she knows this as I have told her myself. She was not that way to me personally but in general. She seemed opinionated and somewhat bossy. Unfortunately, I do not remember when Ruby and I became friends, but she is to this day one of my dearest friends. She is also my photography mentor and has taken me under her wing, taught me some tricks of the trade, told me what I was doing right and what needed improving. She took time during my single days after my divorce, to travel thousands of miles to spend time with me at my humble apartment. We enjoyed some exciting girl time making some memories I cherish to this day. Ruby has been a supporter of most of my endeavors and is always available to offer suggestions, compliments, and constructive criticism.

Shelby was another one of my great friends in Alaska. She and I belonged to a weight loss support group and although we'd engage in conversations, we never really spoke one to another. It was at a hayride she mentioned my petite hands and bone structure and to my surprise, asked my zodiac sign. We began a conversation on that brisk, fall evening that spawned a relationship that is strong to this day. In fact, it was after my trauma in 2009 that I took a getaway to gain composure and went to Orlando where she had moved. She was warm, welcoming, comforting, and kind, yet still offered me the space and distance I needed to get myself together. She has always seen something in me I hadn't seen in myself and been encouraging and uplifting.

Outside of my Alaska comrades, I can only think of a few others that truly stand out in my life to this extent. Sue is one of them. Sue was a military wife who did freelance work from home when I met her. We met when I was separated from Jim for a few months and worked at a local print shop. Sue was a freelance designer for the shop and would bring her completed jobs to the counter where I typically was, and we built a rapport. We had children near the same age and became fast friends. I eventually reunited with my husband and yet through the years, Sue and I remained in great contact. Our military paths never crossed but we personally made it a point to visit and see each other and our families became very close through the years. When I moved to Biloxi, Mississippi I worked as a graphic designer at a local paper and was restricted to use antiquated computer equipment and programs. Mostly because my boss was unaware of what was available on the open market for our industry. Sue, having worked in that field, drove for three hours to discuss the option of him buying her equipment, discs, and programs at a very reasonable cost as she was getting out of the industry. My boss took her offer and the investment completely changed the overall look and productivity of the paper. In past years when traveling, my family and I have stayed at her home. She has been beyond hospitable. When I was speaking in Colorado Springs after the release of my first book, _God, are You listening?_, she drove all the way from New Mexico and spent a day with me just because I was 'on her side of the world' and she wanted to see me. We stayed up late that night giggling like school girls. We laughed, we cried, we shared. And then there have been times when I'm just passing through New Mexico and no matter the distance she meets me to catch up over a meal or a cup of coffee. She is a culinary genius and has written some things for my magazine. I am so blessed we met. I do not think she aware the impact she has had on my life.

Then there is Allie, who at the time was active duty Air Force and truthfully, I cannot tell you how we met. I feel like I've known her all my life. We have children the same age and shared several months of our pregnancies together. I watched the relationship between her and her husband with envy and had the utmost respect for both. In fact, when the military sent her on a year deployment her son was only a few months old and her husband stepped in as both mother and father to hi and their two daughters. Upon Allie's return, she looked upon her son that was now, a year later walking, talking and filled with personality where her baby boy once was. For that long year, her husband was working outside the home, a single father with two young children and a newborn and made it work. They remained steadfast in their relationship and themselves as a couple. Although quite different in personalities and interests our families were very good friends, and we were blessed to be assigned to a few bases near each other in our careers. Allie has always boasted about my talent and giftings, always encouraged me to reach beyond what I thought was my potential. Today, she still supports my dreams and continually offers advice and suggestions to help promote a better product. Her oldest daughter, married with children of her own, lives in the same town I do so when Allie comes to visit them, I get to see my friend again. I love those moments and cherish them.

I could call any of these friends at 2:00 in the morning to tell a joke, share some good news, cry or seek advice and they would all be there for me full throttle. We may not see each other as often as we would like, but when we do, we pick up right where we left off.

chapter six

The Sisterhood and Brotherhood Circle

Although we are given no choice who our siblings will be, we share segments of lives with them. We impact them, and they influence us as well. I have learned over the years, one does not have to be related to someone to consider them a brother or sister. In fact, I have run across many people who are closer and more deeply bonded or connected to someone with whom they share no bloodline than an actual sibling.

But for the most part, after our parents, we are more than likely surrounded and influenced by siblings and other family members the most often in our day to day lives. I grew up the oldest in a house with seven brothers and sisters. I, my biological brother, and sister were blessed when my mother and step-father brought five more siblings into our world. Although not full blood they are as much my brother and sisters as the biological ones and none of us have never considered there to be any distinction in the siblings. My mother's talent and creativity are instilled in all of us simply by being raised in her care and experiencing her creativity on a daily basis. As I detail some of the influences my siblings have bestowed on me, many are more than likely unaware of such an impression.

My older brother Roy is only thirteen months younger than I and has impacted me in many ways. Because I missed too many days in first grade and had to retake it, Roy and I attended every grade from first grade to high school together, graduating in the same class. He was popular and handsome; I was artsy and gawky. And yet he still claimed me as his sister, that alone speaks of his caliber as a human being. Both of us being dark-haired, light eyes with Italian coloring, many classmates and teachers thought we were twins. He has defended me when others ridiculed me, offered advice, and provided heartfelt accolades at times when my life was in serious turmoil. He has stepped up to the older brother role many times. In fact, I recall as a ninth grader asking my handsome, popular brother if he thought I was pretty. He said "I don't know. You're my sister." Pressuring further I asked, "But if I wasn't, would you go out with me? Would you think I was pretty enough to go out with?" The awkward adolescent let out a groan and walked away. Thinking back, it makes me chuckle. He and I have always been close, even though miles have separated us since our teens years. I know he is there for me, whether to leave his friends and walk me to my car or simply send me a note of encouragement and prayer during a difficult time. He has worked the same job since high school, in addition to running several of his own businesses. He builds bookshelves and decks and other things out of wood that are beyond impressive. He has a kind heart, tender soul and is filled with compassion for those he cares about, for the world around him, and makes it a point to be there for those in his life whenever possible.

My oldest of the younger sisters, Sandy, although we agree on very little and are as different as two people can be, has been my rock as far back as I can recall. Even today, I wonder who the big sister is? A few years back while traveling, we were given the uninterrupted opportunity to have a few heart-to-heart, deep discussions. It was in one of those discussions we discovered all our lives we had been envious of the other. Sandy was so beautiful with her golden sun-kissed skin, long blonde hair, blue eyes and long legs, everyone adored her. Yet, to my surprise, she was just as jealous of me because she said, I had "the smile and personality to light up a room when I entered." She has held my hand through difficult times and rejoiced with great enthusiasm during happy times. Sandy has cried and laughed with me until we both almost stopped breathing. She makes it a point to be at all momentous occasions, happy or sad, for all her siblings despite the distance and gives freely of her heart. My sister has joined the fan club of any endeavor that anyone in our family (myself included) is a part of and gives 100% of herself to whatever the cause. She has rebuilt her car engine, reupholstered the interior (including piping around the edges) by HAND, designed and built a chicken tractor (I didn't even know what that was) and is an avid hunter and angler. I tell her she's every man's dream girl! Yes, she is tiny and blond and has flawless golden skin. Yes, I am none of that. However, in our older ages she has become more gray than I, so I must tease her saying, "THAT is God's mercy at work." She has instilled loads of wisdom, insight and been a shoulder and a boulder. I am very blessed to have her influences in my life.

My youngest brother Trace has always been a character, filled with jokes and sass. My first recollection goes to the childhood stories of my mother saying role call as we got in our seats for a trip. Inevitably, when Trace's name got called, he would not answer, making our mother think he was left behind until you heard the giggle from the back seat. After her frustrated reply, a timid "here" emerged. And then there are the infamous words of the song green grasshopper, grasshopper green. which was the ONLY lyric to the song he wrote and sang to us for miles and miles. Exhausting and yet enlightening at the same time, pure boy all the way, Trace often dressed my younger sisters in denim and flannel and took them fishing. To me, he seemed for the longest time to have the heart and soul of a real gypsy, searching for himself. His father, my step-father, was not a good role model and yet Trace owns his own business, preaches to a small rural congregation on Sundays, and has six wonderful, well-behaved, children. He has always been a fan of my art and has many of my drawings framed, hanging on his walls and as well, has dabbled in painting and is blessed with a truly gifted talent.

My little sister Wendy is seven years younger and so full of wisdom. After high school, I left home when she was only ten and have very little memory of her growing up with me. It isn't until our more adult years I have come to know and be inspired and impacted by her. We have children very close in age, as little as ten weeks apart. She is immensely talented especially when it comes to sewing. Like my mother, she can look at something and create the item with no pattern. Also, like my mother, she can make a beautiful home out of thrift store or yard sale finds to the point that people gasp at how beautiful her home is when they cross her threshold. But, when I think of Wendy, she does not know how beautiful she is or that she is an incredible cook. She is the only person I know that can go into a kitchen that to most, literally has nothing to make and create a gourmet meal. She mixes things most would never consider, and somehow it ends up delicious. Although disabled, she has single-handedly raised three awesome children and has taught them the lesson passed down from our mother on the difference between being a survivor and an overcomer.

I recall my little sister Annie, nine years younger, used to be stuck to me like glue when I was in my early teens. My mother made us matching seersucker smock tops, and we wore those whenever we were able. Unfortunately, I do not recall many memories of Annie after I left home from high school. Annie and I also have children near the same ages and have stayed connected and close as we have grown older and she often visited when I was a military wife. Annie is now a pastor's wife, and although we may not see things the same day to day, I can say that in our adult years she has offered me advice, a non-judgmental listening ear and loads of support in any means possible. She is an excellent mother and a wonderful friend. I am proud to have her as my sister.

My sister Polly has always been a unique force in our family dynamic (after me, of course). She is barely five feet tall, and yet every time I think of her, I smile. As a child, she sucked her thumb and pulled her hair until she had bald spots thus leaving my mother no alternative but to force this little girl to sport a crew cut until she could cease the thumb sucking. Of course, the crew cut gave Polly a perfect look for denim and flannels, creating the ideal fishing partner for Trace. Polly is a powerhouse of personality. I recall when she was a young teen, she called my house in San Antonio for an unannounced visit. My military husband and I ended up in the early morning rescuing this cute, young teenager from the unappealing downtown bus station. She was and is still filled with wit, laughter, joy, and spontaneity. I have many memories of her, such as, when we moved to Alaska, greeting us at the airport with a huge welcome sign, attempting Thanksgiving dinner with no microwave and sampling all her edible creations made from whole grains, herbs, fruits, and vegetables. She has five amazing children, one only 3 weeks younger than mine. We shared our "my baby is doing this" stories across the miles during our pregnancies. One of her children received the Honorable Man Award scholarship after high school, two are in the marines, one was born with a cleft palate who underwent numerous surgeries throughout his life. Her youngest, born on September 11th, 2001, and the only of my nieces and nephews I have ever seen born, is also the first baby I had the privilege of witnessing the beauty of on an otherwise lousy day. Though Polly's life has not been easy, she has maintained a giver's heart for her family and others in which she comes in contact. She displays a positive outlook and I am reminded of a time in my life when I was extremely low, and although I do not recall the actual reason or situation for my despair, I remember the impact of my phone conversation with her. Through the other line, she informed me she was going to send me something. A few days later a small white journal with the outline of a blue dove arrived in my mail and a note from her saying: "This is your blessing book. Every day write three things you are grateful or thankful for. You cannot use the same things again. So, you cannot keep being thankful for your family, kids, job, etc. Be creative. Be grateful. Look for the blessings." I did as she requested and was really impacted by this exercise. I started noticing things in my life I never did before like a great parking space or not catching a red light when I was in a hurry, etc. It blessed me so that I have paid it forward and done the same for others.

My baby sister Sarah is the most amazing mother I know. She is currently the only one of us to graduate from college and the only one still married to her original spouse. She is a fantastic person, and even if she weren't my sister, I would be honored to call her my friend. Sarah majored in speech pathology in college and has home-schooled her four children with great successes. She has instilled a way for them to pursue their dreams and yet stay grounded. For example, one of her children wants to be a professional baseball player. Although she has traveled and attended many state and national championships with him and his team across the country, she has also encouraged a plan B and has assisted his talents in learning graphic design programs and techniques. She has one of the most creative designer minds I have ever witnessed and been published in several magazines. I was eleven when Sarah was born, and adopted her as "my" baby. As siblings growing up she referred to me as little mommy and yet I admire her and the mother she has become.

I also have two half-brothers from my biological father and his second wife. Although never raised with them, only knowing them sporadically over the past thirty or so years, I can say that even not being raised with them, they have impacted my life. At first, I admit I was envious, as they had experienced a life I felt I should have had because they enjoyed a loving mother and father under the same roof . They traveled with our father's work learning to fluently speak six languages. They had a father pay for college and buy them a vehicle upon graduation. But I must say despite what could have been a negative impact, these two young men are amazing human beings who have entwined themselves in my life by the love, acceptance and graciousness they have shown. They have embraced my other siblings as family. It's very impressive and I am grateful for them.

I also have some step brothers and sister on my stepfather's side, and whereas my step sisters were decent enough to me, my stepbrother will not even warrant any more words on this paper as his impact was beyond brutal. I have no contact with any of them anymore.

However, when my mother remarried, I gained four stepsisters from her husband. A few I had little or no contact with and therefore little or no impact, but his oldest Joan is the big sister I never had and always wished for. She is kind and funny, and although we don't get to see each other much, we communicate often. I only wish she saw in her what I do. She is amazing!

Siblings, like it or not, are part of who you are. They are your lineage. I was recently speaking with a young pregnant mother who was confident this would be her only child. "He has cousins, so he'll have lots of playmates," she said. Aside from parents who for some reason or another cannot have more than one child, her comment reminded me of research I did when my oldest was born. At that time, I carried the same sentiment. It was in that exploration I discovered not only are most only children often easily engulfed in the realm of being spoiled or catered to but the realization that when my son's parents are gone, he will be all alone. Cousins aside, no one will truly understand or comprehend the dynamic of his life as a part of our family and growing up. I ached for him at that realization and decided he needed a sibling to ensure that through the years, even after I'm gone, they can share stories, memories, influences, and traditions with him in a complete and understanding manner. I am incredibly grateful for my siblings, the impact they have had on my life and the things we have taught each other through growing up together as a family and as individuals. These are things that live on within us and we carry on even after we are gone.

chapter seven
Teaching that Influences

O ur paths cross with many people every day. Teachers, for example, have a considerable impact on our formative years and can leave a profound impression. As someone who attended over 25 schools in twelve years, I have experienced my share of teachers. I will start with the negative influences.

The first recollection I have of an adverse effect came from my sixth-grade teacher in Columbia, South Carolina in the mid-1970s, who kept a switchblade in her desk drawer. The only reason that teacher and that particular account impacted me so was even at my young age, I could not imagine why a sixth-grade teacher needed such an item in her desk. Although I was fortunate never to see her use it, I soon learned of the necessity of having it nearby by merely being a student in her class. As one of only two white students and the only white girl, I was subject to a classroom filled daily with bullying, anger, violence, rage and racial prejudice at an early age. The impressions stuck with me for life.

A later negative remembrance or impact was from a teacher in my junior year of high school. He was the football coach who taught American history for one class a week. As customary for most public schools, a final exam was required and held a majority percentage of the final grade for completion and passing of the course. The final exam instructions were, and I quote: list the names of all the presidents of the United States of America. I began writing, Washington, Adams, Jefferson and so on. I completed the entire list, felt confident I was ready to proceed into preparing for summer, and onto my final year of high school. To my surprise, I got the exam back and received a failing grade of 50. Upon questioning the teacher, he informed me that I did not provide the first names and therefore only received half credit. I politely explained his instruction did not specify first names and I should not be penalized for such. He refused to bend. I had to get my parents involved. Upon a meeting with them and the principal, the coach agreed to give me the proper grade for listing all the names of the presidents. That said, not wanting to feel like I did not earn or deserve something, I stayed after school the next day and recited to him the names of all the presidents of the United States to include first names. The recitation in no way affected my grade, as I was already given credit for completing the assignment as requested. The point is that the teacher's actions impacted me in such a way I felt the need to prove to him I knew the material. This incident often has me wondering if he was affected enough to be more conscientious in his instruction in the future.

I am also reminded of teachers in which I was not the student yet still affected by their actions. My son is a very creative, artistic thinker and when put in the right environment is unstoppable. His fifth-grade teacher is one who he will tell you marched to the beat of a different drum, as she would dress up as historical characters, act out scenes in literature and so forth. She was an exciting and motivating instructor, and he flourished in her class. She saw him as a diamond in the rough and encouraged him to step out of his comfort zone, offering to stand beside him every scary step of the way. She recommended he submit original artwork for the history of Biloxi poster contest to which he won first place, was awarded a plaque presented by the mayor and rode the fire truck in the parade. I wish I could say all educators are that motivating and leave the kind of impression she did.

But, things changed when he started middle school encountering an art teacher with no creative thinking. A typical twelve-year-old boy, although very polite and respectful, was still full of life and silliness. His teacher approached me over and over about his silliness in class and her annoyance with my son that he was not following directions to the letter but doing things differently. The entire situation reminds me of the Harry Chapin song, *Flowers are Red* in which a little boy goes to school making all his flowers different colors in art class. The teacher tells him that is not how they should be. She says to him they should be all red and green, then sits him in a corner until he changes his point of view. Eventually he becomes lonely and conforms. As typical, the boy moves to another school and as he starts to color his flowers all red and leaves all green, this new art teacher tells him to be creative, there are so many colors of flowers. It is a poignant song that still touches me to this day and reminds me of my son's art teacher quenching his spirit and his love of creativity to the point he never did anything artistic again. Her impact made an impression lasting to this day.

An enormous effect on my life occurred when I was in art school. My stent at art school was a very emotional time in my life. Many situations and circumstances forcing me to grow up quickly, facing issues before I should have to, and dealing with emotions I had never experienced. It was while I was in art school that John Lennon died. I grew up listening to the Beatles but was a mediocre fan. However, being surrounded by artists, the day an icon like that dies, is monumental. The school closed for the day as our campus lawns were filled with crying, meditating and somber artistic students. That experience changed the way I viewed the world, and had a tremendous impact on my life and transformed how I related to music from that moment forward.

It was my awards, creative notoriety, and portfolio in high school, that granted me the scholarship to attend a very lucrative art school. The portfolio requirements needed eight mediums and categories in which to provide for one's portfolio. A minimum of three different methods must be submitted to apply. I threw the collection together in less than a month with a designed interior pediatrician's office in opaque markers (including perspective), a self-portrait was done in charcoal pencil and a slideshow of various mediums including paper artwork and clay sculptures. I had no expectations of being accepted due to my lack of preparation time and skill set. Besides, there were over 500 applicants from around the world applying; the school had a reputation of accepting only 50 per quarter. However, I was accepted.

I worked hard and learned a great deal. One of my classes was a typography class where we learned about lettering typestyles. Our semester assignment which covered a large percent of our final grade was to create a circus poster. We could use any medium we were comfortable using. Towards the end of the semester in this class, my roommate was raped one night on her way coming to our apartment. It was difficult for both of us as two single women living alone. In dealing with the rape issue, I feared to go to class and remained cloistered in my apartment, worked daily for extended hours on my assignment, and consoled my roommate. My roommate dropped out of school, moved back to Minnesota with her parents, and I eventually had to find another place to live, as well as venture back to classes. I knew if the assignment was late, it would be dropped a letter grade but was confident it was the best work I had ever done. I painstakingly had put in hours beyond the norm to ensure it was so. Attending the grading class that day, my instructor placed all the posters around the room and one by one analyzed each one, pointing out the qualities and the flaws. I knew in my heart my poster was at least B work and so even with the late penalty, I was sure to receive a C. My instructor, however, gave me a C, with a final grade of a D. I was beyond devastated and met him after class. I recall telling him that work was the best thing I'd ever created in my entire 18 years of life. I explained in detail how many hours I had worked, how I perfected the hand-drawn letters, so there was no warp on the edges, how the opaque watercolors were the perfect consistency, not too watery and not so thick the colors cracked. I asked why I received the C and ultimately the D? He informed me, "I only have you three hours a week. I do not know that this is the best you have ever done. I can only compare you to the other students in the class and their work." Now mind you, there were people in that class that were as old as my mother at the time, and many were on their second or third art school. I wondered how I could ever compete. That grade ultimately led to me losing my scholarship and being unable to finish art school but the impact it had on me personally, professionally and as an artist was astronomical. I learned about comparison and competition that day. I never considered myself competitive and didn't prefer to be anything other than my best self, but through that experience, I learned that sometimes your best is not enough. This incident put a ridiculous standard on my personal and creative self-worth. This decision, complied with my roommate's rape and her untimely leaving school, caused me to live in a paradox between being a closet perfectionist versus merely doing my best work possible.

As far as other educators go let me give you another view. A view from the outside looking in. While in my late forties and early fifties, I was privileged to be a substitute teacher for a Georgia county public school system and was primarily placed with elementary students with special needs. I often transported them to various classes.

It was during one of those times my heart was crushed along with the spirits of two children. The first was a little boy in third grade. The short version is the vice principal came to the door and asked for him by name. Door still open, she stood with the child in the doorway and said leaning over this young man, {Mr. Smith}, (pointing to the teacher sitting at his desk) said you were disruptive in class yesterday. I want you to apologize to him. As the teacher began walking to the door, the child politely tried to explain himself as others were involved and instigators, but the principal interrupted, pointed her finger, raised her voice, and made her demand louder. Other children witnessed this reprimand, as well as myself and the child I brought to the classroom. It was at that moment I saw that little boys countenance fall, and he looked up at the teacher with his hurt face and said, "I'm sorry, Mr. Smith." That moment impacted me, and I was merely a witness. I can only imagine the repercussions it had on that child. I believe, yes, children need to learn, and as adults, we are here to teach them. In word, action, and deed. I personally felt the principal could have handled the situation differently by at least taking the child in the hall privately and not humiliating him in front of his peers and strangers. She could have listened to his side, allowed him a voice, and an opinion. She could have used a kinder, more loving tone and perhaps motivated him differently. All those impacts may have had a different outcome in how that child grows up to be and how he sees himself.

The same day, in the same classroom that same teacher, Mr. Smith, sat at his desk while the students were doing work. A little boy came to his desk, folded colored paper in hand and said, "Mr. Smith, I made this for you." The teacher put his pencil down, opened the card and while the child was stood right next to him, the teacher threw it in his wastebasket in plain sight of that young boy and said, "Go sit down and do your work." The boy, head dropped, turned around and returned to his desk. My heart broke, and I wanted desperately to tell that teacher how that youngster must look up to him to give him such a piece of his heart like that. I wanted to remind that teacher of the courage it must have taken the small child to muster the strength to make such a gesture. I wanted to ask him why he chose a teaching profession in the first place. But most of all, I wanted to rescue the crayon covered card from the trash and tell the teacher he should at minimum have thanked the boy and if he intended to toss the card, done it after the class was over and the boy was gone and not while in the child's presence. Who knows what that child might have been enduring at home, what made that teacher have such a significant impact on him? And the moment, the anticipation, the intentions, were tainted by one single act. Perhaps it was the impact of the experience with my stepfather throwing my poem away in my childhood that made my heart ache for this child.

Now let me share with you the opposite side: educators who influence positively. When I was in fifth grade in Escondido, California, I was a very gifted, busy student, reading teacher's books from the library, in addition to having what is now known as ADHD. School work was often dull, and I was a daydreamer and would often do anything to get out of my desk. But I was creative, loved teaching, and helping others. My two teachers, Mrs. Agetep and Mrs. Wilson, saw through my challenges and tapped into my strengths. They allowed me to assist other students with their school work and tutor them. They used my creative artistic talent to create the multiplication table for the bulletin board. I sat with poster board, ruler and markers and not only utilized my skills but was able to stay seated for the entire class times until it was completed.

Mrs. Agetep had an angel broach she often wore on her blouse collars. Only about 2 inches wide, gold colored, and displayed a flying angel blowing a trumpet. I loved that broach, the sparkle, the way the angel held her trumpet while flying. It was the prettiest thing I had ever seen. The beginning of October, Mrs. Agetep approached me with a sheet of graph paper and a challenge. She explained to me every square represented a day of the week I would be in school. At the end of each day, she would offer me an X or a gold star for that day, depending on how many times I got up from my desk unnecessarily or was disruptive. If by Halloween, I have more stars than X's, I would receive her broach as a special prize just from her. The excitement of receiving that broach led to motivation, which ultimately led to victory, and I did earn that broach. I also stayed in contact with both teachers until their deaths in the late 1990s. Often they would send me photos from trips, and if I recall correctly, Mrs. Wilson made Teacher of the Year before she retired. Eventually, the trumpet broke off my angel, but I had that broach well into my forties. I think she got lost in one too many moves. But those two teachers impacted my life in a significant way, and I have utilized their method of teaching with my children, substituting and tutoring others.

As well, I recall my art teacher, Mr. Hemsworth in tenth grade, insisting I submit works to the state art show. It was his motivation and belief in me that ultimately led me to obtain two state competition awards at a special award ceremony. He saw something in me, my talent that I had not seen, and I blossomed as a result leading to art school three years later.

My drama teacher in high school, Mr. Thigmen, was that rare teacher who stands out in a crowd. To him, drama was not about acting and school plays, but about art, expression of self, and so much more. I recall once in class he played Bob Seger's *Night Moves* and asked us to close our eyes and listen to the words. When the song was over, we were each to tell him what picture played in our heads. It was quite the exercise. For one of our assignments, we were to find a song and perform it on stage. He was the reason I wanted to be an actress and change the world through the example of the way I lived my life.

As a substitute teacher in a special needs class, I was assigned to a second-grade class for two weeks while the teacher attended a training conference. One boy, Luke (name changed), who struggled with ADHD, also had issues at home, of which I did not know the details. Although given the daily lessons and schedules for the two weeks, I was not given the assignments for who is line leader, door holder, calendar person, etc. I took volunteers and had one spot left for the calendar. I nominated Luke, and he adamantly refused. One of his fellow students informed me to the group, "Ha! Luke won't do a schedule. He doesn't do that." At the time I let the issue go, left the slot blank and proceeded with the daily activities.

While other students did their work, I called Luke to come to see me at the desk. I asked him privately why he didn't want to do a calendar. He said, "It's stupid; everyone looks at you, and if you do something wrong, they laugh." I informed him there would be no hurtful laughing or teasing in my class. We were all there to learn, and I would prove that to him. I also mentioned how great he was to be selected to do a calendar. You get to be the teacher for a few minutes. You get to ask what day of the week it is, what month, year, and what the weather is outside. In fact, YOU get to pick who goes and looks out the window to give you the weather. His eyes got big, and he cracked a smile. I reassured him I would be right beside him. He agreed to do it. I told him to keep it our secret, not mention it to the students and see how proud they are when I call him up on his day. He agreed.

Later that day, I left a sticky note under his book that said, "I'm proud of you. You're going to do great!" He saw the note and smiled but didn't look at me. The day before he was due to be the calendar student, I reminded him before he went home on his big debut tomorrow and told him to get a good night rest. The next morning, after the students put their backpacks and lunch boxes away and formed their semi-circle for calendar time, Luke sat among them as usual. I called him up, and the class gasped. You could see the pride well up in this child as he took the pointer from me and pointed to the calendar asking the various questions. He was a natural and did a great job. And there was no laughing.

About two days later his teacher stopped in after an early day from her conference to get something from her desk. Asking the students and me how things were going, one student said, "Luke did the calendar." Stunned, the teacher looked at me and said, "How did you do that? I can't get him to participate in anything."

I like to think I had an impact on Luke, motivated him to see his self-worth and helped him learn how to conquer his fears in life. Teachers and educators are making an impression every minute of every day. If you are in that career, I commend you. But I also challenge you to be aware not only of the little minds you are shaping but also of the influences you are leaving behind.

chapter eight

The Imprint of Apostles & Heroes

Pastors and outsiders can often impact us, negatively or positively as well. As a child, we were not a church-going family until I was about sixteen. As you may have read in _God, are You listening_? my step-father became a pastor during my later teen years. Although the experiences with him were not pleasant, the involvements with others created memories and influences that are positively embedded in me for life. My step-father was without a doubt one of the most charismatic, impressive speakers I have ever heard, but he did not live the life nor possess actions that displayed what he spoke.

The pastors at our first church in Columbia, South Carolina were amazing, encouraging and uplifting to this lost, scrawny teenager. I attended the required catechism class for our denomination and enjoyed many Myrtle Beach retreats. In the course, we did more than learn denominational doctrine. We took trips to other faiths and shared services with them. We were taught to accept their beliefs and respect their differences. One trip was to a Greek Orthodox church, where we experienced the ritual of incense while the entire service was sung in Latin. I remember the robes lined in gold ribbon and the crucifix as they were things in which I was not accustomed to seeing in my church. However, having been prepared and informed about the proper protocol impacted me to this day as a believer that we all share a belief in something, and that although different than what another may believe it still warrants esteem and homage.

Our youth retreats showed me the power of campfire songs, a sense of unity, togetherness, and freedom to be your true unencumbered self. I learned how awesome it is that the same Creator that designed the magnificence of the mountains, the beauty of the mighty oceans and the splendor of the galaxies looked at me and thought the world needed one of me in it also. One of those retreats taught me I.A.L.A.C.O.L. (I am lovable and capable of loving) and has served as a remembrance many times in my life and has been something I have shared with others. Since those days I have reunited with a few of those pastors in my life, informed them of their influences and the molding they made on me as a person.

However, being a preacher's kid automatically comes with a confusing stigma. You're either a tramp (because your family is so strict that you're rebellious) or you're too naive, sweet, and innocent, and no one wants to hang out with a goody-two-shoes. People tend to make this judgment call about you on their own with no input or personal knowledge about you as an individual. It was however, when I met a few young men, from various back road country churches in Virginia, who really changed my perspective on humanity. These boys were a typical country song. Living in love and off the land, without a penny to their names or a care in the world. They sang around the campfire and made me feel like I was the most beautiful girl they had ever seen; they thought that I was too pretty and too special even to be seen with them. They relished any moments we got to hang out together. These young men taught me at an early age that people are what is inside. Outer appearances are typically either showmanship or insecurity but rarely genuine or original. However, to be true to yourself and KNOW you have something to offer from the heart is the greatest gift of all. We were more than friends but shared an innocence that movies are made of. I still have the letters Don and John wrote to me. But unfortunately, not too long ago I found out they were both killed in a car crash. I regret I never really told them how special they continually made me feel or the impact that had on a homely, insecure girl.

I think we can agree positive role models are imperative to the lives of children. I've always said it is essential for children to have other role models in their lives besides their parents. Rare is the boy who grew up with a father who didn't like the outdoors or sports but had an uncle or in-law who took him fishing or threw the football until their arm nearly fell off. It is in those moments impressions are made, life is taught, and lessons learned. Somehow, they also seem more valid when they don't come from a parent. I have experienced some of those in my life.

My pastor in Alaska for example was, to me, one of the truly great heroes. Not only a good preacher but also a great teacher as he painted pictures with his words and used everyday situations to make his point to teach how the Word of God pertained to life today. He was real and transparent, even from the pulpit. I was blessed to work with him at our church for many years and was part of the firsthand dealings and heartfelt decisions made on the staff level. Pastor Tom had the heart to serve. He wasn't a pulpit pounder but managed to get the message across. He believed in fellowship, in walking the walk, not just preaching a message, and talking the talk. Pastor Tom genuinely cared unconditionally about others (in his congregation or not) and was as sincere and honest behind closed doors as he was to his parishioners. Although no longer pastor at that church as he battles Parkinson's disease but his transparency, unconditional, unjudgmental love for all and the strength behind his humility still influences me across the miles.

As a kid, I recall my aunt Cheryl, my mother's only sister, for whom I am named after, serving as a great reminder of divine impact in my life. Without being overbearing in her preaching and beating us over the head with a Bible to get the Word in us, she was the epitome of grace, patience, and unconditional love. She talked the talk AND walked the walk every moment of every day. She was without judgment and full of love; her heart was huge and giving to anyone and everyone, no questions asked. As children, when she would come to visit our family, she offered us each a dollar for every book of the Bible we'd read. No pressure to learn but the offer was there. She never pounded into us, "Did you read your Bible?" or "What books have you read? Don't you want to get some money?" Nothing. Just simple subtlety. She appeared among the meek, yet I recall her screaming at the top of her lungs one time in the backyard for Satan to leave her and her family alone, spouting that he had no authority over them and he must flee. In fact it was at a revival she took my mother and me to when I was twelve years old in which I discovered my own personal divine encounter that left an impression on me to this day. It is still so real when I think of it as if I'm right back there. I was wearing a mustard-colored velvet dress with   eyelet cuffs on the sleeves. We were standing at our pews, and the pastor is fired up about giving your life to Jesus. The church congregation is filled with organized chaos, tears, laughter, singing, dancing, and praying. Being unsure of my surroundings, the outcome or anything, I stood between my mother and my aunt, holding on to the pew and looking down at my hands. It was then I noticed a stain on my sleeve. It bothered me, so I put my hand behind my back at the exact moment the pastor asked for anyone who wanted to give their life to Christ. I guess my mother thought I raised my hand because she took me to the altar with her. To say that moment and that visit with my aunt impacted my life would be an understatement. Through the years my aunt has taken unwed mothers into her home and helped them get education, jobs and on their feet once their babies were born. She has run several nonprofit businesses and to this day, despite her ongoing battle with Lupus, has taught me and others about true grace, mercy and love as she still takes every step in the footprints of the Lord.

My Uncle Rams, my mother's only brother, was a highly decorated Vietnam Veteran. It wasn't until my older years as a military wife for twenty years that I understood and appreciated all that came with the title Vietnam Veteran. Uncle Rams is a recipient of numerous military honors and awards to include but not limited to National Defense Service Ribbon, Combat Infantryman Badge, Bronze Star Medal with OLC, Gallantry Cross with Bronze Star, Army Commendation Medal for Heroism with V device Air Medal, and Parachutist Badge. I warmly remember his visits when I was a teenager. He usually pulled up in his leathers on his motorcycle. Uncle Rams was well known for being very handsome, and although I was a teenager, I never saw him as anything other than my favorite uncle. He would offer us kids motorcycle rides around the block. Except for me. I got to go for a long ride, get ice cream, and stay out longer. I never found out why. Maybe he recognized the looked of someone's eyes when enduring a life of personal unexposed pain. Uncle Rams had a way of making you feel like the most important person in the room. In his older years, he came to visit my military husband and me in Alaska and shared many trips down memory lane with us.

Easing the pain of all that being in Vietnam held, alcohol was his best friend and ultimately cost him two marriages, many jobs and eventually his life at an early age. But the day of his funeral, in a room filled with family, friends and motorcycle club members, I remember one man standing up and saying how every Friday night my uncle Rams was at the VFW telling people about Jesus. Not in a pushy way but as he said, picking up a book he brought titled "The Ragamuffin Gospel" by Brennan Manning, "He shared this book and his story with me, and they both changed my life." That was how I remembered uncle Rams too. A flawed human being, broken yet filled with love, compassion, and a deep appreciation for grace. It was through sitting at that bar, and his unconditional love that many learned about the unconditional love of Jesus. What a legacy to leave. I miss him greatly.

My grandfather on my mother's side was an Army veteran and a podiatrist. He was also a man of great faith. He routinely held Bible studies in a detached building off his house he proudly called "the Jesus Room." When I think of memories and impacts from my grandfather I am immediately taken to a car ride. Once riding in the car with him, we saw a bumper sticker on a vehicle in front of us that said, God is my copilot. He asked me, "What's wrong with that saying?" Dumbfounded, I shrugged my shoulders. Grandfather explained to me that God is our PILOT, as the orchestrator of everything in our lives. WE are the co-pilot. In my lifetime I have seen that sticker many times since, and it always brings my grandfather and that conversation to my memory.

My grandmothers were many. As I mentioned before, my mother's parents had both remarried and so growing up I had two grandmothers on my mother's side. My grandmother Lura, my mom's stepmother, married to my biological grandfather, was always kind to me as a child. In 2017, she transitioned to her place in heaven, and as I attended her celebration of life ceremony, many memories were brought back to my mind as I roamed the very house I remembered visiting as a child. A few things really stand out about my grandmother, Lura. I remember going to visit her and my grandfather. She would take me to the base and we'd go shopping and have lunch. I felt so grown up and special. In my late teens, when questioning her about my biological father, she said she never met him but knew of him and the stories. She dug through old photos and provided me with a photograph of my mother and father and me as a baby. That gesture gave me a sense of belonging and purpose. Later in my years, she gave me an amethyst ring of hers she wanted me to have which means even more to me now that she is no longer with us. It was the something old my new daughter-in-law wore on her walk down the aisle.

My maternal grandmother was very special to me. I was her first grandchild, and we had a special relationship. I was her moon child and never did I see her that she didn't squeeze me tight and kiss my cheeks. Although I do not recall many visits or outings with her she never ceased to make me feel wanted, loved and special when we were together.

These people were heroes to me in some form or another. Through action, deed, or merely being real and genuine, they touched my life and left a permanent imprint that I carry with me every day.

chapter nine

The Influence of Others

My grandfather had children by three different wives; therefore, some of my uncles are younger than me. My Uncle Thom is one of them, as we are only five months apart to the day. As children, we were very close. He was a chubby kid with big glasses who played in the band, and I was a homely, skinny, pale girl with first-born child responsibilities and a huge insecurity. Thom and I shared many dreams, secrets, and ideas as children playing together. At five years old, we pretend-married ourselves to each other under the big oak tree in my grandfather's (his father) backyard. Feeling like no one would genuinely understand us like the other, we dedicated our lives to being there for each other forever. In fact, I recall in my late teens moving back to Florida and needing a place to stay until I made enough money to get a place to live. Thom offered me a safe haven at his apartment with his roommate. We picked up right where we had left off. Distance never seems to keep us apart.

In my early twenties, I relocated back to the town where Thom and I spent most of our childhood and Thom still lived. We spent a lot of time together, even dieted together. I remember going out to eat and ordering a pitcher of water before anything and splitting it before we would order any food in hopes that we would be too full to eat our entire meal. Often, we were each other's dates for outings, concerts, and events. I recall him picking me up to attend a square dance and ending up in the wrong place - An O'Jays concert. We kept each other accountable, were not afraid of the ugly truth and appreciated a compliment from each other.

In our fifties now, Thom lives in the Midwest and me on the East coast. The last time we saw each other was at my Uncle Rams funeral. I was thrilled beyond words to see him and hug my uncle and my dear friend. He holds a special place in my heart and has impacted me in many ways, I don't think he even realizes.

My Uncle D was married to my biological aunt for over 35 years. He suffered from emphysema, and it eventually cost him his life, leaving my aunt beyond devastated. When I think of Uncle D, I think of a saint. In all the years of knowing him, spending time with him or being at their house, I never heard him yell, curse, or even get mad. But he was not a wimp. He was a strong, hardworking man, with deep morals and a huge heart. Every time I'd call on the telephone, he'd say, "Hey, girl. How ya doin?" I cannot think of a single time we ever parted that he did not tell me "I love ya' girl." He was filled with love and generosity and made my aunt happy. She is an intense, strong-willed, loud, independent, Italian woman so, yes, he was a saint.

My Aunt Jae has played a considerable part in my life since meeting my biological father at age 16. She considers me the daughter she never had. The woman is so impressive, I wrote a two-page article about her in my magazine. As I have gotten to know her and held close intimate conversations with her, I discovered she was Salutatorian of her high school class, that together she and husband housed, clothed, rescued and raised seven children, many from the foster system. She has volunteered for a crisis pregnancy center for nearly 30 years and was awarded the George Bush Award for Volunteerism. She fosters stray dogs and is a Respect Life Minister at her church. As if any of that was not impressive enough, she has impacted me personally as a role model and friend. She has offered advice, constructive criticism and unconditional love to a once-estranged niece.

Another person of influence in my life was a maid we had when I was about nine. I remember Thelma as a hefty lady of color with a heart of gold and weird medical practices. One of the things I remember is some of her homemade remedies. It was during that time the Thelma was with us that I had a boil on my rear-end. My mother tried to no avail to pop it, but as you know, fanny skin is difficult to get a grip on and apply pressure. Miss Thelma told my mother to boil an egg. Once boiled take the skin and separate it from the egg and the shell, place it over my boil and cover with a band-aid overnight. The next morning Thelma laid me over her knee, removed the band-aid and with a slight stroke of a fingernail across my boil, shot the entire infection including the core, all the way to the ceiling leaving a blood spot. She was filled with remedies like that and many of them I have carried with me in raising my own children.

chapter ten

Teaching Teens

I would consider from age twelve to seventeen the formative years, at least it appeared that way for me and my children. It was during those years many influences were made and remained in my thoughts and memories. I have already highlighted a few individuals who impacted me during those years but would like to touch on this period a bit more specifically. As you know, I was not a preacher's kid until around age 14 when my stepfather joined the seminary. Except for the occasional Sunday church visit with my aunt, I really do not recall being a regular church goer before that time; however, a few pastors stick out in my mind. During our mandated youth instruction, we had several pastors who influenced in positive ways by the way they lived and conducted themselves.

Quite contrary to what I was experiencing at home, they provided a sense of hope and knowledge of what was more normal than not. Recognizing we were curious, vivacious, young men and women, I recall they instructed and yet were not judgmental. They provided answers and were open and honest without being pulpit pounders. Some of our youth leaders were a mere few years older than me and in fact, I remember one I had a serious crush on at the time. Knowing this, rather than exploit an opportunity, he was moral in his actions and yet did not shun me or make me feel unwanted in any way.

In my children's lives, many were the times youth pastors were a haven or confidant in which to speak freely on issues and things that perhaps our children felt could not be discussed with us, as parents. These positive influences, I believe, save lives, as I have known of many circumstances such as adolescents who have contemplated suicide and confided in a pastor rather than a parent. The impact of this relationship is monumental. The right positive influences can be instrumental in a teen's life, and as parents, I feel we need to embrace those individuals that we respect, and our teens admire.

As teens, we also enter the workplace and are introduced to a life of responsibility, routine, and unselfishness. In my lifetime, I had more jobs than any one person should. Although a great worker, dependable, loyal, and devoted employee, I never really seemed a fit to any position I held. My first job was working at an ice cream store, and I had to take the city bus to and from there. I did not learn to drive until my early twenties, so all my jobs until that point either required walking or public transportation.

One of my most influential positions was at seventeen when I was an assistant manager at a small retail boutique. Often, I walked six blocks at night, after the store closed with the bank deposit on me. The bank was near my apartment, and I would drop it off on the way home. It never occurred to me to be afraid. I was merely doing a job. It was also at that position I had to approach an employee, whom I'd caught shoplifting and fire her. I did not want to leave that impression on her and was as kind and understanding as possible.

Co-workers can have a tremendous effect on our job performance, self-esteem, and overall impact us negatively or positively. Having to fire a co-worker was not easy for me as a 17-year-old, but as a boss, I knew it was a necessity. I have had co-workers who didn't like me and tried to get me fired merely because I did a good job; perhaps they felt my quality work ethics made them look bad.

I have been in management most of my employed life and always treated my employees as family. In fact, I have hired family. But to me, being family does not mean you get preferential treatment, nor do I expect more out of you than I do of others. I simply expect the job at hand to be done correctly and with pride. I have never been above asking my employees to do something I would not do myself. In that regard, most of the time, my employees respected me, came through when I needed them, and went above and beyond as that was the legacy, I was showing up in MY work. I living by example.

As a teenager we are emotional, hormonal beings who are confident we know everything about everything and yet somehow, we manage to grow and mature to realize our parents were usually right. We begin to learn about the opposite sex, our own sexual needs, wants, and desires and the way we are influenced by situations, circumstances, and our peers regarding them. Our first real break-up is often the end of the world as we know it and we feel we may never survive, and yet, somehow, we do. Our relationships during our teen years often mold us and shape us into our adulthood. These relationships, if negative, can build up hurt, resentment, bitterness, fear, pain, doubt, and many other emotional bindings and scarring that we often carry with us into our adult lives and relationships. Yet, how beautiful that the opposite happens if we are influenced with positive role models and adults who impart love, compassion, understanding and even constructive criticism in our lives; who believe in us and our potential despite our ignorance, stubbornness, and pride.

My greatest childhood friend was Maggie. Maggie and I knew each other since I was nine years old. She was the baby of her family, with two older brothers, and went to a different school than I did, but lived right down the street. She often spent more time at my house than hers and was part of our family. We shared everything. Even in all my moving, Maggie and I remained best friends. She would come to spend summers and school vacations with me and my family. To this day she is spotted in many of our family photos and vacation pictures as we dig up old albums and scrapbooks. We have not seen each other face to face since my mother invited her to my 21st birthday as a surprise. We have both grown up, moved on, raised families and lived lives without the other. But our friendship remains a tender memory in my heart. She lives in

Texas, and I live in the South, but we are still connected and often communicate on Facebook.

About age 16, there was Tanya. Tanya was who I wanted to be like. She was the most popular girl in school. All the boys, including my brother, adored her. She was cute, funny, and smart. I began to mimic everything Tanya did, attempting to be all that I saw she was: popular, cute, funny, and smart. Henry was a cute boy who had a crush on Tanya, but she had a boyfriend. My goal was to be so much like Tanya that Henry would like me, and I was determined to be noticed by him. Although Tanya and I were acquaintances, had some classes together, and went to the same church, youth group functions and so on, we were never friends or hung out at school. In fact, to this day, I'm sure she has no idea how much she influenced my life at that time. Henry, on the other hand, impacted me in such a way it held on well into my adulthood. It was Christmas break, he showed up at my doorstep, envelope in hand. I opened the door and my heart sunk. Without saying a word, he handed me the envelope and walked away. I, of course, was ecstatic. Inside was a small school picture of him. He DOES like me. I thought to myself. My heart was fluttering, and I was overjoyed. Until I turned the photo over. On the back was written, "Go play in the traffic. Harry". Those words crushed me and my spirit for many years. Even as an adult, the piercing words of an adolescent engulfed me and with every failed relationship I asked myself, "What was wrong with me? Why was I not worthy of love?" That photo remained in my school memories album well into my forties when I finally decided I did not need to hold my self-worth hostage any longer. I threw it away finally.

Then there was James, a preacher's kid, like me. His father taught at the seminary my stepfather attended. He and a few other instructors' kids, Steve and Marty, Erik, my brother, and I were all about the same age and were huge skateboard friends. James was beyond brilliant. He skipped several grades in school. In fact, in his casual everyday conversation, he spoke like Sheldon from the television show *The Big Bang Theory* and often very serious about most things. One night while babysitting Steve and Marty's baby sister, I received a phone call from Erik asking if I'd heard that James had hung himself a few hours prior. I had not and thought

Erik was playing an awful prank. Convincing me he was not, I was devastated.

Erik came over to be with me and help with the baby, as he knew I was distracted by the news. We were informed that James and his mother got into an argument. He went to his room, slammed the door, and turned on his music loudly. It wasn't until his mother sent his five-year-old sister to get him for dinner that anyone knew what transpired. The effect of James's suicide hit me on so many levels that day and remains with me still. See, as much as James and I were friends, I often avoided talking to him very much, and when I did, I kept my conversations short because I felt inferior in dialog and didn't want to appear stupid or have him feel like he couldn't carry on a regular discussion. It was at his funeral the emotional floodgates opened even more than before for me. His service was an open casket, as a scarf was placed around his neck like an ascot, to cover the rope burns. He laid there looking peaceful surrounded by the many photos and flowers. Leaning against a memorial arrangement was his skateboard. Someone noticed the bottom of his board had a drawing on it. Flipping it over, we saw it was a drawing of me. That day I found out how James honestly felt about me, and I had in my own way pushed him away out of my own insecurities. At sixteen, I learned a huge life lesson - sometimes the impact we think we have on others may not be what it truly is. James will forever be in my heart and knowing him has changed the way I approach people daily.

In my ninth-grade year of school, my best friend was Mari. She was incredibly beautiful, and all the boys loved her. She was spunky and sweet, long blond hair, and smile that lit up a room. I was none of that, and yet, we became the best of friends. She attended youth group retreats with my church group, and we had sleepovers with many great times. Mari encouraged me to set out to find my biological father and was there when I made the call. She played the mediator for me as my father and I wrote letters. He would send them to her address, and she would bring them to me at school, so I could read them. Then she would hide them at her house. We could not risk my step-father finding out I was communicating with my real father. Having reconnected over the years through Facebook, she told me how much I inspired her with my faith despite everything I had endured during that time in my life and, yet she inspired me as well.

For the two summers between my junior and senior years in high school, I was a camp counselor in Virginia. At sixteen and seventeen, I was responsible for six young girls between the ages of eight and twelve-years-old for an entire week for every week of the summer. I would get a new group of girls each Monday, and they would leave on Saturday. Week after week, the girls impacted me more than I think I did them. But beyond that, I was touched by many of the other counselors. One became my summer romance, another my best friend, some others my confidants and many others I stay in contact with still to this day. But they all hold unique influences in my life affecting who I grew up to be.

Ken was my boyfriend my senior year of high school and a few years after. He was a grade behind me, so we went to two proms. Of course, as most high school romances go, we were in love and had made plans to get married and go to college. I graduated and went to art school a few hours away and visited nearly every weekend. I had a promise ring on my finger, and we relished our plans, the life we would create, and the children we'd raise. Then Ken graduated and went to college about the time my college pursuit was coming to an end due to lack of funds. Although still in the same state, we had merely switched roles; he was off to college, and I was living in our hometown again. Still, I drove nearly every weekend to see him. As time went on, schedules crossed, and fraternities infiltrated our lives, we eventually broke up. For almost four years our families were entwined; Ken's and my lives were wrapped around each other's every move and decision, then suddenly we went about our separate lives. I am still in contact with his sister and stay informed about him, his health and happiness. But I find it ironic how innocent involvement changes so quickly because of environmental and personal influences that enter our lives. Perhaps it is the universe, or fate, or something entirely unrelated, but I know now as an adult, Ken and I would not have been right for each other and therefore, I'm content to hold on to the memories rather than the actual man.

As I mentioned earlier, in high school I was mostly an artsy nerd, very creative and smart. I was also an honors student and Who's Who Among American High School students for both my junior and senior years, which led me to have friends who were more on the other end of the spectrum: the artists, thespians, geeks, scientists, mathletes, and such. Although I did have friends who were cheerleaders and jocks, my people were the freaks, the dreamers, the searchers. We would gather on weekends to sit by the water, play guitar, sing, and look at the stars. For some reason, I have always connected better with males than females. My senior year in high school Ken was my boyfriend, but my best friends were guys, too. These guys protected me, loved me unconditionally and accepted me for my quirky self. Whether they wanted to get in my pants or not, it never came up as I was one of the guys and we were all friends. I watched my first Rocky Horror Picture Show with them, went to Grad Night at Disney World together, one took me to homecoming when my date ditched me, and others helped me move after art school. I still have contact with them to this day. So, to Mark, Mike H, Jan, Mike S, and Andy, you guys totally rock! Thanks for taking a chick like me and including her. Your impact and love in my life are permanently embedded.

chapter eleven

Workforce Infiltration

I 've already tapped into a little of the employment influences and experiences in my teen years, but I'd like to continue further into my adult life, as there are some crucial instances that have influenced who I am today.

As a military wife, I worked a lot of jobs, not because we traveled a lot but because, as I mentioned earlier I had difficulty finding a fit wherever I worked. But with what an airman made in the late 1980s, I had to work to make ends meet for our family. When we lived in Texas, I worked for a garage door company. I was 28-years-old, and the owner was hiring an office assistant. The job seemed simple enough, and I was hired on the spot by the owner himself and offered an above average wage.

Mr. N, in his early to mid-fifties, was a sweet man. He seemed lonely yet had a photo of his wife on his desk. Most days Mr. N came in about 11 am, coffee cup laced with liquor if he came in at all. A few days into my position and to my surprise, I realize I was the entire company. I oversaw general office duties plus taking garage door orders from customers, ordering the doors from the various manufacturers, scheduling installations and maintenance, dispatching calls to our servicemen, problem-solving, payroll (including my own), accounts receivable and payable and more. In fact, there were days I cleaned up vomit and a man passed out on his desk. But in the two years that I worked there no one, customers, employees, vendors, or Mr. N had any idea I had no experience in garage doors. I ran that company.

Mr. N enjoyed talking and it seemed like he needed someone to listen. I lent a willing ear many days when the workload would allow me. He confessed to me his wife left him due to his drinking. He loved her, missed her dearly and daily. I heard him often talk to her wedding picture on his desk. When he'd take trips down memory lane, he'd mention her and speak fondly of his grown children. He often said he was going to win his wife back, of course, he said this while drinking vodka from a coffee cup. The job itself had significant meaning and purpose for me because I felt a sense of obligation to keep the company running and not let him down. I cared a great deal for him, tried to support and encourage him to try sobriety and possibly win back his true love. Working for him had a tremendous impact on me.

Several years later, I received a call from his wife. She found my number in the office files while she was cleaning things due to his untimely death, and the business had gone under. She informed me while driving drunk, he ran his car off a cliff, and died in August. Ironically, I wrote this poem in June 1989 a few months before not knowing of his passing:

the retched lines of a lonely face,
the coffee cup that's vodka laced,
the notes that are unreadable,
the days that seem unbearable.
the memories of wedding vows,
of answering children's who's and how's.

the business that is crumbling,
the brittle legs are trembling.
the lack of will, so twisted still,
the cup still laced, the heart misplaced.

all reasons for your pity.
all reasons for your sorrow.
you own a thousand good excuses,
but you don't own tomorrow.

what will those who love you do,
breathe easier, or cry?
for all the answers you sought in your cup,
we ask each other why?

without considering those around you,
you selfishly made your choice,
and now, though you're no longer here,
there's memories of your voice.

but memories are all we've got
and all that you clinged to.
but now you're gone and i'll be damned
if i'll start drinking
and wind up lost like you.

~~~

Then there was Richard J. The only man who I can honestly say was the closest I ever had to a father. His picture sits on my desk to this day. He was a man of faith, with deep-set values and family roots.

Hiring for a graphic designer, I walked in his business one hot Mississippi July, and he showed me the desk and the small seven-inch Macintosh SE computer in which I would build the tabloid newspaper. He asked if I knew the program. I had print shop, typesetting with layout experience, and had grown up at the feet of my mother in marketing and advertising my whole life, I felt confident I could do the job. I was hired on the spot and told me to come in on Monday. In truth, I lied to get the job and said I knew the program even though I had never heard of it. On the way home, I stopped by a local bookstore and bought the book with the intentions that I would read it over the weekend. Little did I know the book was written almost in computer geek and I had no idea what I was reading. But I went in Monday and faked my way through.

Richard J sat with me and showed me the ads he'd been building, how to store, back up, find, change and so forth. Most of the ads had text and a logo and were, in my opinion, quite dull and blah. I remember the first ad I built was for a clothing boutique. I found a piece of clip art with the drawing of a lady leaning. I propped her arm on the name of the business. I showed it to Richard and asked what he thought. At first, he was skeptical because it was out of the company norm. "Fax it to the customer and see what they say," he said. Well, the customer loved it, and within no time I was dubbed miss magic fingers, and Richard J would bring me a copy and simply say, "Do your thing."

I worked for Richard J and his family for nearly ten years as their principal graphic designer. He was a proud Cajun man from Lafayette, Louisiana with five children. His wife would bring us lunch often, and our meals and breaks were often family style around the large break room table. His oldest daughter, Dolla, was the office manager, son-in-law Ron was in sales. Also, he had a typesetter for the classified ads, a person or two for the front counter, and me. We were a small office with significant productivity. The paper was a weekly issue and came out on Thursdays. That meant Tuesdays were our stay and work until it's done nights, then off Wednesday and distributed Thursday. Many times, my son had to sleep under my desk because my husband worked a night shift.

Richard J was full of advice and always willing to lend an ear or help in any way he could. I recall many occasions, I would walk into his office with a problem of any sort, and he would have a solution. Once he loaned me money to get a tire when we had a flat before payday and let me pay him back over several paychecks. In ten years, my family became intertwined with his. In fact, Dolla is my daughter's Godmother. Several employees over the years came and went, and a few times I had assistance in the graphics department but nothing permanent. My family became part of his family. We shared Thanksgiving together a few times at his camp in Alabama filled with s'mores, four wheelers, children's laughter, and bunk bed stories. It was genuinely momentous times.

But, Richard J, a relatively young man in his early 50's, was diagnosed with congestive heart failure. We were all very protective of him, his activities, and his diet. But what started out as a typical day on November 3rd, 1995, ended in tragedy for us at the paper. We were getting things done as usual. Customers were coming in the front door, salespeople, including Ron and Richard's baby daughter Dyna, are getting their stuff gathered to get on the road and the back end is busy rearranging the office to make it more efficient. Tables, chairs, and the copier were all being moved. "Move your butt, Me-shell," Richard J says to me as he reaches to slide the copier from beside me. I look over and noticed he looked weak, pale, and out of breath. As he grabbed the counter and sat down, I asked if he was okay. I immediately called Dolla from the office. Upon seeing her father, she then ran next door to get her mother. By the time they returned, Richard J was on the floor with me beside him. His wife gave him a heart pill and commanded someone call 911. Lying on the floor, nearly unconscious, she asked if anyone knew CPR. She did compressions, I did the mouth to mouth for almost half an hour before the paramedics arrived. Upon arrival, with him beside me, the paramedics worked on him for a long time. We were all crying, and I remember saying to the paramedic next to me, I know he's just an old man to you, but he's everything to us. Please. Unfortunately, Richard died in my arms that day and my world got darker.

The holidays that followed were not the same with him gone. The next four years were turmoil. Not just from a business standpoint and trying to function without the brain of the vision but personally. Everywhere we turned was another reminder, another part of him that lingered making our mindset of trying to continue productivity come to a halt.

But after nearly a decade of working for this family and being a part of its growth and its heartbeat, my husband and I were reassigned to Alaska. I was tasked to find my replacement. His youngest daughter Dyna was in sales at the time and sat with me periodically and would observe me in the ad building process. Because of our military assignment, I trained Dyna to be my replacement. She has been the graphic designer ever since taking the publication to new heights. I am still in connection with the family. In fact, we just lost Ron last year and Richard J's sweet wife a few months ago. We stay in touch with whatever is going on in our families, even though miles separate us.

Even now there are many times I hear Richard J's voice in my head, or the advice he would give me, a little phrase he would say, or the *"Listen to Richard, you'll never go wrong."* I often think about the Cajun way he would pronounce some words, like my name. I wish he were still here to offer advice and, as an entrepreneur myself now, I reminisce about his small business tactics paying homage to the way he provided for my family all those years, as well as the caliber in which he ran his business. I wish I could tell him one more time how much he meant to me and the impact he had on my life.

Here is a poem I wrote for him after his death:

when i think of him, i think of
hank williams senior,
carmelites and faith,
wondering if he's watching me,
from behind those pearly gates.

strong enough to stand up
for whatever he believed,
a dedicated hard worker,
never ashamed to roll up his sleeves.

yet, gentle, kind and caring,
the most unselfish soul,
all these things make up the man,
that i've been blessed to know.

like pinching pennies and hunting,
zydeco and farfetched dreams,
happiness and contentment,
and cajun legacies.

the glimmer in his eye and a pat on the back
made everything okay.
but when i think of him i wonder,
if he thinks of me today?

when i think of him my mind explodes,
with all the man possessed,
and i pray that God will watch over him,
until i am His guest.

~~~

His children, Ron and Dolla, were an inspiration to me and impacted me both as a couple and as individuals. Only a few years older than me, Dolla was beautiful, spunky, caring and yet strong and tenacious. She ran the office for her father and handled all the financial and human resources aspects of the business. Ron was the leading salesperson and was very much a people person. With his good old boy, Cajun personality you couldn't help but love him. He was small in stature but big in the heart. The story was told to me like this. Ron met Dolla when he was 18, and she was 13. Ron was the guy in school who smoked, skipped class, etc. and Dolla, well, she had Richard J for a father and siblings watching her every move. Ron liked Dolla, and Richard J wanted no part of it but seeing that this was a losing battle he took Ron aside and told him Dolla was not allowed to date, but he could come to the house and visit and hang out on occasion. Richard J also expected to see Ron's report cards and informed Ron that if his grades were not acceptable, he was not allowed to visit. It apparently worked out because Ron and Dolla got married when she was 18 and were married until the day he died, forty-something years later. They lived together, worked together, worked for her father and yet not one time did I witness any strife within that family dynamic. Their son Lane was a year younger than my son and their daughter a few years older than my daughter. Our families hung out together and shared birthday parties, Mardi Gras parades, camping trips and so forth. She still runs the business and has been an essential part of its growth over the past 30 years.

Dyna, the youngest, experienced some poor choices during part of the time I worked for her dad. But I watched her father rescue her from the toxic situation she was being swallowed into by offering her a sales position. No longer the spoiled one, Dyna was raising two daughters close in the age to mine, living with her parents and working for her dad. Although younger than me by ten or so years, Dyna and I quickly became good friends and as mentioned earlier, she loved to watch me create the ads and would often dabble in helping when she had extra time. While working there, I was able to witness a young, messed up girl grow into an independent, strong woman and homeowner. Before I left for Alaska, I attended her wedding to a military man whom she is still married to nearly thirty years later. Her girls are stable, strong women and although not close in miles, we remain close in heart, and I am very proud of her.

Both our families have endured much through the decades in which we've been separated, but we stay connected through social media and are acutely aware that any of us is only a phone call away. In sickness or health, tragedy or triumph, we are a family.

chapter twelve

Impacted by Illness

Illnesses and diseases have a way of touching us that we never honestly expect. We have all lost someone to cancer, heart disease, or other debilitating illnesses or tragedies. We have watched them slowly deteriorate and leave our lives as they leave this world. It is heart-wrenching and impressionable. I have already mentioned a few people who have impacted me and my life who have transitioned their worldly bodies to the great mansion in the sky. They all have left a hole in my heart, and a part of my world lacks luster without their presence. Yet, the impact they have moved within me allows me to continue their legacies and shine on in their honor as I tell their stories and remember them.

As I look back on those I've known and loved who've struggled with illness, I realize my memory bank is full. Yes, there have been far too many. Most gone too soon while the memories overflow. I have already shared a few with you in previous pages but would like to honor a few ladies that have left a permanent impression on me the way I live my everyday life.

First, there is Kathy. Kathy was my mother-in-law for over 25 years. Divorced, overweight, raising two boys on a less than small salary, she lived in a falling apart, rented trailer and could hardly afford her necessary bills, let alone any luxuries. But Kathy loved me. I married her son. I took him out of a life of failing college and partying to the military, where he blossomed in a 20+ year career and obtained a bachelor's degree and 2 masters during the years we were married. Kathy and I shared loads of time, laughs, and moments together over 25 years. The last time I saw Kathy was at her mother's funeral. Though years had passed, she did not recognize me. In fact, Kathy asked if I knew her two sons and wanted to introduce them to me. At 55, she was suffering from onset dementia. Over the past several years she has progressively become worse; talking to her is like talking to a four-year-old. Her condition has forced her boys to put her in a care facility for her own safety. She was my mother when my own mother wasn't around and always seemed to love me unconditionally. Although at the writing of this book she is still with us in the body, the Kathy I knew and loved is gone, and I miss her greatly.

When my ex-husband and I retired from the military, we set our sights on buying our first house ever. I visited the area we were retiring to and met a fantastic real estate agent named Angie. Angie drove me from house to house for an entire weekend. If memory serves, we looked at over 30 houses in two days. Having to get back, we agreed to keep looking, and Angie would send me house listings. Angie had a husband who did not value her and sought the company of someone much younger. Angie and I shared many of the struggles of dealing with divorce and feeling like unwanted goods. She has remained a good friend and confidant over ten years later. I no longer reside in that house or that area, but Angie and I do remain friends, stay in contact and get together whenever I am in the area. Unfortunately, she is suffering from cancer and fighting hard. She is a wonderful mother, grandmother, and overall inspiration to anyone blessed enough to know her. I know I am blessed to know her and call her my friend and excited that she is doing well and is engaged to be married.

Then there was Iva. Once divorced, I moved to another city and became a certified nurse assistant providing in-home care to patients in the area. Iva was a beautiful 80-year-old woman. Once a pilot in the military, and then one who circled a helicopter overhead and did traffic for the local radio, she told me many adventurous stories of her life, despite her progressive dementia. She lost her husband early in their marriage and was never able to have children. However, she spoke highly of memories of her ex, the adventures they took, and their life together. She loved to sew, garden, and cook and was not accustomed to sitting idly by and letting someone else do for her that which she felt she was able. As her dementia progressed, so did her frustration. We made many memories like reading together, dancing in Winn-Dixie while grocery shopping, taking walks in her neighborhood and watching Wheel of Fortune every evening while eating Dulce De Leche ice cream (that was her favorite) before she retired to bed. As her caregiver, watching her was both heart-wrenching and eye-opening having me wondering about my own aging. Iva was phenomenal in so many ways and yet struggles not only with the disease itself but in her own personal effort of doing what she thought she can do versus what she indeed can do. That is horrific to watch as a caregiver.

Even at my age now, I struggle myself with bouts of "where did I put my keys" with small memory lapses and I wonder what my own mental status will be like when I am an 80-year old woman. And since my mind never sleeps, this has me thinking and reflecting on her as well. In composing a list of things I hope my caregiver will be aware of, I found it ironic how Iva's and my paths are similar and how our needs, dreams, desires, wants, and frustrations are as well. Perhaps that is why I knew I was right where I needed to be in that job. No, the money wasn't the greatest and the hours, not the best, but the rewards were tremendous. I can only hope that when I am her age, someone will also take the time, care, patience and compassion to truly understand not only the disease but the person who struggles to still reside within it.

For my caregiver when i'm older:

i may be losing my mind but i'm not losing my memory.
each day i remember things i used to do and love and so to help
us both remember who i still am i share these reflections:

i am creative in many ways and so i don't like to sit idly much,
i prefer to stay busy.

i like to be outside.
i don't have to walk or dig in the garden (although i do enjoy that)
but i do enjoy just sitting and listening to nature - perhaps you will
take a moment and sit with me?
i don't watch television, much prefer a good book or a sketch pad
or journal.
i love to take pictures and really see God's canvas that
is all around me and capture that.
i am a social person and enjoy those interactions with others.
i need to be needed.
i love to cook.
i am passionate about many things
and need a purpose to get up every morning.
i love to laugh and need it often.
i have a story to tell and a heart full of love and tenderness.
my confusion is as frustrating now
as losing the car keys was once.

please be patient with me in every way.
life is too short to rush through anyway.
try to remember that it's difficult for me also,
to relinquish every aspect of my life to another
when i have always been so independent.

grow with me.
enjoy the journey.
learn from it,
for one day it may be yours
and you will also be making a list
of all the things you love and who you are.

~~~

Then there was Tracy, a young single mother. If she were 30,
I'd have been surprised, raising three children under the age of
six. Tracy's middle daughter was in my Sunday school class. She
shyly participated but was outspoken and very creative. Tracy and
her children lived about 40 minutes from the church and about an

hour and a half from my family. It was at a trip to Walmart that I ran into Tracy with another lady from church, named Angela, who informed me they were there to get her some makeup before she started Chemotherapy, so she could draw on her eyebrows and have some color in her cheeks, etc. I had no idea until then that Tracy was diagnosed with breast cancer. While Tracy was occupied with the task at hand, Angela communicated to me that Tracy's husband had left when given the news, as he had lost a previous wife to cancer over ten years ago and simply could not handle the situation again.

Tracy, an elementary school teacher, was in good spirits and seemed optimistic whenever I saw her at church dropping her daughter off. As months passed, I saw her turn thin, pale, and her hair diminish. I coordinated with Angela to get to Tracy's house on Friday to clean, do laundry, change bed sheets, and make a one-pot dinner that could be tossed in the oven. I wanted her weekends to be filled with time with her children, not household tasks. It was my plan she would come home from a long day at school, plop the pan in the oven while she got baths done, and then all sit and have supper together. With the rest of the weekend for fun and enjoyment, not laundry and dishes. The first couple of weeks Angela assisted me, but then I was solo. As months went by, I was cleaning increasingly more hair out of Tracy's tub drain and seeing more and more prescriptions by her bedside.

She had a double mastectomy and was not afraid to share her triumph, showing her scars to me and using them to encourage her children in her fight. But unfortunately, Tracy died on Mother's Day that next year. Her children were, as expected, devastated but her daughter in my class was questioning why God would take her mother, especially on a day dedicated to remembering one's mom. Knowing her mother allowed me to explain to her daughter that her Mother's Day memory did not have to be about her death but about all the memories they made with all the good times they shared. I feel this approach made her look at that day a bit differently and I believe it had an intense impact on her view of every Mother's Day since. I know it did to me.

chapter thirteen

Brief Encounters

A s I am sure you have gathered by now, the people we encounter impact us and us them, in various ways. Whether positive, negative or merely a brief passing of glances, words or nods, a meeting of sorts has been made. Often, we go about our day, not even realizing the effect such a situation might have created until the moment it manifests.

For example, I worked in retail for most of my teen years and even into my adult life after my divorce. In that industry, as well as in a supervisory role, I dealt with people daily, often one on one. I helped locate items, solve issues, or just engaged in conversation. It was one of those occasions when I was putting some stock on a shelf and a regular shopper, we'll call her Mary, approached me about an item she was looking for. I escorted her to the area we carried them but explained to her I believed we were out of stock. She was convinced we had them as she was there the day before with plenty on the shelves and was sure they could not all be gone that quickly. Upon approaching the area, we noticed the shelf was restocked with another item. She questioned that perhaps there were just a few left and they were placed someplace else in the store. She followed me to numerous locations in which the item might have been relocated. Noticing she was becoming aggravated and having difficulty walking, I offered her to stay still and let me do the roaming.
Upon final knowledge that there were no more of that item in the store, I offered to call another store and see if they had the item.

She continued to become even more hostile and the tone of her voice extra abrupt, despite my diligent and generous efforts. She became extremely rude and stormed out of the store in a huff, muttering obscenities. Several months later, however, she returned to the store. She came in as always, did her shopping, paid the cashier for her items and on her way out the door spotted me. Bags in hand she approached me and said, "Excuse me. I owe you an apology. I was in here a while back, and you graciously helped me look for something. In fact, you went out of your way, and I'm pretty sure I was rude and nasty to you. Not that this is an excuse, but I had just started a diet the day before, but my blood sugar was low because I had fasted for my doctor's appointment, and I hadn't eaten in over 24 hours. Plus, my head was throbbing, so I had very little patience. You were very accommodating, and I wanted to say I'm sorry I was so awful." Of course, I accepted her apology, and the impact that apology had on me made such an impression on me, well, that it made it into this book.

Seriously, how often do we treat someone badly and then ask for forgiveness? Or even yet, how often do we think people are mean or rude and not consider they may be going through something we know nothing about and offer a little extra kindness and courtesy? People are emotional, and we often run on those emotions. This lesson, this one brief encounter had the potential to remain in my memory as a mean and nasty impatient woman, who didn't get her way but ended up being an act of forgiveness, a humble apology and it taught me to offer a bit more grace where emotions are concerned.

Another moment that comes to my mind is that of a peddler who rang the doorbell on our parsonage house when I was about fifteen or sixteen. I recall his hair was long, black and stringy, his face unshaven, and had a sock hanging out of the open fly of his tattered blue jeans (which I found very odd). Although he was intoxicated, he appeared harmless and had a gentle spirit about him. Someone who approaches a pastor's house in need is more than likely filled with the expectation of unconditional love and gratitude and so my mother being a true pastor's wife, invited him in, offered him a shower, a meal, and a clean set of clothes. But before sending him on his way, she invited him to attend church with us the following Sunday. Much to our surprise, he showed up the following Sunday looking for our family, dirty clothes, matted hair, and alcohol breath, he stood out front waiting for us. Unfortunately, parishioners gave glances, passed him by, even overlooked his very presence until we showed up where he was invited to sit in our pew with us, and did. That is when the whispers began. Following the service, he asked my family if we could take him someplace. He said that he needed to get something. Upon our arrival at the location, he took my mother and showed her an antique barrel, hand crank washing machine that he wanted her to have as a gift. It was the only thing he owned of any value, and he wanted her to have it for her gracious hospitality, generous heart and a welcoming spirit.

My mother could have not opened the door that night. The man could have not come to church the following Sunday. But one act leads to another, good or bad, a ripple effect happens. Impacts are made every second we encounter another human being. We never saw that gentleman again after that, but my mother had that old washing machine, sharing that story home after home, state after state for many years. I'm sure the story alone impacted the people who heard it.

Brief encounters often happen without us realizing it. Sometimes people are brought into our lives for a mere moment, but the memory lingers, and the impact remains infinitely. Like for me in 1979, at the Ringling School of Art and Design campus. There were several of us new freshmen hanging out and getting to know the campus, the other classmates, comparing schedules, etc. Off to the side, I noticed a young man, tiny in stature for a man his age, with blond wavy hair and a guitar strapped to his shoulder. I went up to him and said, "Play me something." Without hesitation, he pulled his guitar around to his front and began strumming the strings and singing *"Time, after time. I sit, and I wait for your call. I know I'm a fool but what can I say, whatever the price I will pay. For you, Madame Blue."* That is the first time I ever heard that song or those words. Now mind you, I was from the generation and was very familiar with the band Styx who originally recorded the song, but I had never heard that song. It was his voice and his passion in singing and playing that moved me in such a way my mind still wonders where he is 40 years later, what he's doing, which brings me to the impact words and music have on us.

chapter fourteen

Musical Moments

Words, especially in music impact us often in ways we never realized. How often have you heard a song that speaks straight to your heart or says precisely what you were trying to say but couldn't find the words? Better yet, how many melodies do you hear that bring you down a path of memory lane? Have you ever said, "That song reminds me of?" Like you, I have many of those but here are a few that I'd like to share: *"Right Down the Line"* by Gerry Rafferty always will bring my 11th-grade crush Tommy B to mind. I was a junior and Tommy was a senior. We were friends but nothing more. Darn It! But Tommy loved that song, and I loved Tommy, so now every time I hear it, I think about that schoolgirl crush. I've confessed my undying childhood affection for him as online buddies and enjoyed a pleasant stroll down memory lane. But Gerry Rafferty and Tommy B., they just go together nowadays.

When Richard J, my pseudo father died, Vince Gill's, *Go Rest High on That Mountain* was out and very appropriate during that time frame for me. To this day, I cannot listen to that song all the way through without crying. I most assuredly cannot hear it without thinking about Richard J and his influences on my life. I miss him. There are also many songs that remind me of my mother. As I recollect on my childhood and adolescence, I am reminded how my mother was always singing, to us, with us. Sam Cooke's *Summertime*, Bob Dylan's *Don't Think Twice It's Alright*, Joan

Baez's *The Night They Drove Old Dixie Down* and *Delta Dawn* were all songs she sang to us in our youth. As we got older, we shared songs like *Take Me Home Country Roads* by John Denver, *Cool Change* by Little River Band, and anything off the Carol King's Tapestry album brought memories of her since we know nearly every word to every song on that album.

Good, bad, sad, memories, moments, music and lyrics hold keys to many aspects of our lives. My college roommate Lindsay and I were roommates for a short time, and she played guitar and loved Jackson Brown. We used to sing his *Stay (a little bit longer)* together, and it always brings me to our humble little apartment in art school. When I hear David Bowie's *Fame*, it makes me think of Don and John as they used to sing it around the campfire at our church outings. When Ken and I broke up, I was, of course, devastated. As I lie on my bed sobbing, *Lady Down on Love* by Alabama played on the radio, and at the time it was as if the writer was peeking in my window at that very moment. That song embedded itself in my soul and I am brought back to that memory every time I hear it.

You can see by these few examples how music speaks to us in a plethora of ways. But in taking the trips down memory lane or embracing the lyrics that are precisely what you wanted to say, have you ever considered what it is about those lyrics that impact you? Have you ever really examined the thoughts, feelings, and emotions they stir? I have heard stories of a suicide attempt intervened by a song on the radio that spoke to the victim and provided hope, peace, and/or a will to live. Recently, my daughter was going through a bad situation in a relationship, and she kept listening to "I love you, don't leave" type songs. It seemed only to be making her sadder and more depressed. Someone suggested she listen to some "good riddance, you don't deserve me" music. Once she changed her playlist, it completely changed her attitude, mood, and mindset. Often, especially in music and poetry, we are influenced by things around us in which we are unaware we have control. If we really examined the thoughts, feelings, and emotions, we may find that we have the power to determine our destiny and our successes.

There are so many songs I can say, was our song about a relationship that no longer exists, or they played this at my senior prom, or I sang this at my school's talent night and so forth. Whereas many lyrics expose pain, love, heartache, and healing, often some are viewed to exploit abuse, hatred, and division. Many musicians are aware of the magnitude of their words and are conscientious of the legacy they may leave behind. For example, the well-known rapper Will Smith once said he will never record anything he would not want his mother to hear. Perception, I suppose, is everything. What is perceived as a certain way to one culture, or age group may be completely different from another. So where can we draw the line between artistic freedom and maintaining awareness and consideration of perception of others? Should we even try?

Music impacts everyone individually. This was made clearer to me the other day when I was driving in the car with my 19-year-old step-son when the popular song *Hello* by Adele came on the radio. "I like this song," I said. "but they play it too much." He said, "I think its creepy." I asked, "Why do you say that?" He proceeded with, "She's called him a thousand times. That's bordering on stalking. Obviously, he doesn't want to talk to her." I laughed, and said, "She's just thinking of him and wants to say she's sorry things ended badly. Apparently, things didn't end well, and she wants to connect with him." "Well, I still think its creepy," he said. Giving more thought to this music theory mindset, I asked a friend of mine about the song a few days later, and she agreed with my step-son. It just goes to show that the same thing can impact different people differently.

chapter fifteen

Short Term, Deep Impact

Quite often someone comes into our life but for a brief season and then for whatever reason, they are no longer there. Customers, peers, long distance relatives and so forth. Yet their impression leaves an immeasurable mark on us that sticks like red wine on crisp linen and therefore, they live as a part of us for the remainder of our lives. They impact our thought process and for whatever reason influence our decision-making.

As an Air Force military spouse for over twenty-five years, of course, I encountered many people. Many of these people earned this distinction of Short term, Deep Impact. The unity and camaraderie of a military community are like none other I ever experienced in all my growing up in gypsy-style traveling years. Perhaps it was because we were all within the same rank and therefore, income bracket, or maybe the sense of unity was due to our kindred spirits of understanding of where we'd been and what we'd been through. Many of us were married couples, in our late teens to late twenties. We barely knew much about each other and yet we trusted one another with our children, used each other as our emergency contacts, gave keys to our homes, and combined cupboards to create a balanced meal between our families. Some of these couples and families I have maintained contact through the years. Others, as typical with the military, lose touch after many transfers, and even Facebook doesn't seem to have a profile on them. But the impact remains. The sense of belonging, the unconditional trust and the freedom to be humble without judgment are immeasurable. It is a lifestyle not for some but comforting and comfortable to others.

As well, weddings and funerals often bring people into our lives briefly. Of course, surrounded by family and friends, we are presented on these occasions to meet new individuals we may not otherwise have met, friends of friends or distant relatives. These opportunities are available for you to reach out and make an impression, shine your light, reach out to someone and perhaps touch a life.

I often speak about funerals and question the motive behind waiting until someone is gone to tell a room full of people what they meant to you. I find it best to do so while they are alive. As mentioned in some of my other works, I began to wonder why we wait until someone dies to say the good things about them. And then we gather in a room filled with other people who also knew them and probably knew the same or similar things. Why? Why not when the people in our lives are alive today?

I once attended a retreat where letters were written by various people who knew the attendees, and the letters were then dispersed to them at a special dinner. It was a very emotional time, and those letters still hold unique significance for each of us. For one attendee it was the last and only letter ever received from his father, as his dad died only a few months later unexpectedly. I challenge you to take the time. We live in an electronic age where we send hundreds of emails a week. Why not send one person in your life an email a day? Tell them what they mean to you TODAY. Tell them the good things they bring to your life and the things that make them spectacular to you. The smile that lights up a room, the personality that is full of energy and makes them a joy to be around, the faith that moves mountains whatever it is, why wait to tell strangers what this person has done to your life? Tell THEM. I did this myself, and I can tell you it is not an easy task. If you REALLY search your heart, it's almost like writing a eulogy but in present tense.

I encourage you to make the time because you never know how much time anyone really has. We indeed are all works in progress, and I believe, deep down, we all need the encouragement to know we are living a life of purpose and meaning, making a difference. Maybe my opinion of you doesn't make up your self-worth, but it's still nice when I hear the good things I bring to your world, to your life.

So, again, I challenge you to open your email address book, get out your Facebook friends list and start making a list of good things. Share them while people you care about are still alive to appreciate it. Who is first on your list? Your action in taking a moment, making a small gesture, could leave a huge impact, leave behind a legacy in which you and those you leave behind could be proud.

chapter sixteen

The Impression of Perception

Throughout this book, I have touched on various ways I personally have been affected by people, their words, deeds, and actions in my life and in some cases, given examples on how perception is often different than what it appears or was intended. I have proposed ways for you to not only be aware of your daily surroundings and the people you meet but to make a conscious effort to make an impact in the lives of everyone you encounter. From the cashier at the store to the voice at the other end of the phone line, how different would we react if we continually remind ourselves they are someone's child, mother, father? What if, instead of reacting with frustration and impatience, we simply reached out with kindness or a smile and remembered the impression we are leaving at in that moment of their story? Especially if our children are with us, always watching, learning, discovering how to react, respond? I encourage you to consciously live every day in every situation with the intent to leave the legacy you want your children to live out with their lives.

At thirteen years old my son had a mentor friend in his youth group who was eighteen. This friend would often stop by our house to see if my son wanted to go to the movies or get pizza with some others. One moment was an evening around dinner time when this young man stopped by. Opening the door, I informed him we were just sitting down to dinner and invited him to join us. Sitting around the table, he asked, "Do you guys do this every night?" I said, "What? Have dinner?" He responded, "Eat at the table as a family. My family never does that." He went on to explain that his stepfather was an alcoholic and his mother worked two jobs to support them. Our nightly routine made an impression on that young man. Perhaps for the moment, maybe for life. As was often tradition, at our dinner table, we played what we called, the high-low game where everyone had to state something high and something low about their day. As parents, we felt this initiated conversation with our teens and allowed us insight into their worlds. We included this young man in the ritual that evening. Perhaps he thought that my son had a perfect life because he had parents that sat around the table and cared about his day. The truth was that our marriage was struggling, but through the trials we dealt with, we stayed true to our children and their well-being; because of that I can confidently say that the simple gesture of a meal around the table made a significant impact on that young man that night and possibly to this day.

Curt was one of my son's best friends in high school. Although not in the same neighborhood, they lived close enough to walk to each other's homes. Curt lived with his older brother and dad, who worked a lot trying to make ends meet to support two growing young men. The boys were often left unaccompanied, and it was common that Curt was at our house often for days, even on school nights. I was never the kind of parent to fuss at my children and send their friends home. If they both did something wrong under my care, they both were reprimanded. I treated Curt the same as my son. In fact, I talked to them both about girls and so forth. To this day Curt is still considered my other child.

At one point, I carpooled six middle school boys after school and had the opportunity on many occasions to impart some wisdom to them from the driver's seat. Now mind you, middle school age boys are already awkward enough merely by their age, dealing with enough identity and life situations at that age. As well, they are just young men, so the selective hearing gene is already developing, but I like to think I imparted a few words of wisdom occasionally. As an example, John, an only child, was a rather quiet, shy, and withdrawn young man, but he and my son were friends at church. His parents didn't have much financially, shared a beater with a heater car and lived in a house that needed repairs they could not afford, but from my perspective, John always seemed to have what he needed. His parents worked hard to provide a good life for him. Chad on the other hand, also friends with my son, was from a very affluent family. Money seemed no object for them. They had a 7,000 square foot custom built house with a guest wing and game room and Chad often boasted on his upscale lifestyle. Chad, on the other hand, lived with his mother, step-father, younger brother, and baby sister. Whenever possible, he spent much of his year traveling to visit his biological father in another state. I made a circle in my drop-offs from the school to various houses of the boys that eventually ended up with the last one near my home where my son and I would finish our commute. Chad lived closest to the school, so he was dropped off first. It was at a moment that we pulled into the driveway of Chad's beautiful home and he got out, politely saying, "Thanks for the ride." As I watched him walk to his door, John sighed and said, "Chad is so lucky. I wish I had his life." Looking in the rearview mirror, I saw sadness come across his face as this young man compared his lifestyle to his value as a person. Driving off, I immediately spoke up and said, "John, as lucky as you think Chad is, you have something he doesn't. Something he will never have." John's look back at me was of confusion and wonder, excitement, and intrigue. "What do you mean?" he asked. "Chad will never have both of his parents living in his house together; to share his day, to see him grow, to watch daily as he grows into a wonderful young man. He may not be able to talk to his step-dad the way you can talk to your dad, and his mom and dad do not share a love for each other as yours do. You are blessed that you have both of your parents with you every minute of every day." John looked at my eyes gazing back in the rearview mirror, and he said, "I guess you're right." I like to think it planted a seed. If nothing else, a seed of appreciation for his parents and the love they had for each other. Unfortunately, John's father died in a car wreck about three years later. As expected, he and his mother were both devastated by the untimely loss.

Perception can be tainted or transformed. As we spoke about with music, the way we see things may not always be an accurate assessment. Often it is beneficial to get a perspective from someone looking from the outside in, as we are often too close to see clearly. I am reminded of another situation in my early twenties when I worked at a very elite designer boutique. Although permitted to sell throughout the entire store I was specifically assigned to the men's department. I recall working alongside a 40 something African American AME preacher, Vern. Vern worked part-time to supplement his church salary and help with his family's finances. He and I were great friends, shared many stories, and life lessons in our downtime on the floor. Vern always had wisdom for my young ears and mind. As a preacher, he could tell stories that were captivating and impactful. I could ask him anything no matter how racial, inappropriate, or naively it may be received; he always had an answer for me, no offense, no judgment, just forthright honesty with transparency. One of the greatest things I recall about Vern was a little antidote of advice he would give me. All these years later, I still remember it, and whenever I say it I see his head bobbing and his big smile grinning, filled with attitude as he blurted out the words: "It's good business in the line of business to find you some business of your own. And if you ain't got no business, then make it your business, to leave my business alone." Kind of catchy isn't it? It still makes me smile. Little thing, significant impact.

Then there is Elliot. When I met Elliot, he had just started dating my friend and was at her birthday party. He was polite, helpful, and had a huge smile that lit up the whole outdoors. However, little did I know, until he and my friend got married a mere four months later, that Elliot had an addiction to heroin. To say the first year of their marriage was hell on earth would be an understatement of epic proportions. Between the constant home police visits, bouts of domestic violence, verbal abuse, credit card fraud and destruction of property, I was in a steady state of fear, aggravation, and exhaustion. I quickly grew to not like this young man at all and was convinced Elliot clearly was not the husband I had wished for my friend as described in the Book of Ephesians. These obvious feelings caused tremendous tension between my friend and me and made gatherings awkward and visits scarce. But then something changed. My friend got pregnant, and before the baby was born, events occurred which caused Elliot to be court ordered to attend a local 90-day rehabilitation facility. This program allowed him no contact with the outside world for the first 30 days, only approved visitors on certain days for a limited amount of time for the next 30 days, and no cell phones or computer access for the entire duration. As my friend's pregnancy progressed, Elliot was still in the program the day the baby was scheduled to be born. Due to his behavior, cooperation and overall attitude, the facility agreed to allow Elliot to be accompanied two-hours away, strictly for the birth of his child. I was there with him and my friend as we stood by her side. He was nervous, excited, and scared. I saw a tidal wave of emotions barraging his face throughout the delivery process and into the actual birth. It was at that moment that I saw Elliot in a different light. He looked different. Sweet. Genuine. Human-like. Not the monster I'd remembered. He returned to the facility after the birth of the baby and upon completion of the program, reunited with my friend. They worked together on rebuilding their family and their relationship with each other. Elliot got a job, was looking into starting college, and had bought a brand new car. They had a daily routine and regular family outings and even better, had plans for their future. Our families also shared some meal times together. I was starting to kind of like this charming, fast-talking, Cheshire cat smiling guy.

I'd like to tell you everything turned out wonderful, and they lived happily ever after but unfortunately, at 27 years old, Elliot unexpectedly died in their home late one evening. My young friend never dreamed she'd be a widow at age 24 raising their baby alone. Who knows why anyone is taken before their time, and there are still questions in which we may never have the answers. But, at his memorial service, as I reflected on a mere six months prior and the year I had just concluded, I realized that knowing Elliot had a considerable impact on me, on many of us. For at the funeral, we all had the same type of stories. But I was able to pull out one thing confidently. Elliot taught me, my friend, and my family how to love the unlovable. He taught us about second chances and believing in the impossible. He inspired us to learn what it means to never give up on someone. There is no way to know if Elliot would have stayed on his upswing path or not, but I believe, his daughter coming into his life saved his life. Even if for a few months. Unfortunately, she will not know her father in a personal way, but we will all be reminded of the efforts he made, the chances he took, the unconditional love he had for her and the impact his presence had on our lives in such a short time.

Yes, relationships, even short encounters can impact us in various ways. Some for good, some not so much. But it is often our perception that cultivates our impressions and makes the impact.

When my daughter was about nine, she had a friend Shelly. Shelley's mother, Dana was a single mom. She and I were also friends. Dana would often bring Shelly by, and we would visit while the girls played. She would make a note of things like my home, my husband in the kitchen cooking and my general lifestyle as if she coveted the life I led. What she didn't see, despite my telling her otherwise, was a home created with yard sale and thrift store finds, a struggling marriage and a genuinely unhappy person sitting beside her.

Perception can be defeating. If we tell ourselves, we are less than adequate, then we are. If we compare ourselves, our lives, our children with others then we are doomed for failure. For no two people, experiences, children, or situations are alike. I once heard a saying that I remind myself of often when I get a defeatist attitude toward myself. It says, "Your playing small does not serve the world." I try to tell myself every morning when I wake up, "Somebody needs what I have today."

chapter seventeen

The Wisdom of Innocence

C hildren impart such wisdom at nearly every encounter. I have heard that sometimes you need to talk to a three-year-old to understand life again and I believe this to be true. As a tutor, special education teacher, and oldest sibling, I have learned a great deal from the children in which I have come in contact. Simple things like sharing, kindness, living life full of curiosity and wonder, playing nicely, and hugs from your mom are the best. There is something about the innocence of children that gives them the right to be free to express themselves without hindrance, to say what's on their mind and to be appreciated for being genuine.

My daughter was born quite the leader, and that has not changed. In first grade, she was the little helper. Some call it bossy I liked to think her strong will and take-charge attitude would make her a good leader someday. I wasn't far off. At a mere 24 years old, she is a mother of two, a registered nurse and 1/3 into her master's degree. I recall her first-grade teacher telling me, "She's a better teacher than I am."

As adults, our innocence can be ignorance, and the impact not what we'd hoped. We can impact others unintentionally merely by not being confident in ourselves, our talents, and our knowledge. For example, that same first-grade teacher taught the children that using an X for the word Christmas was to take Jesus out of Christmas. As a child raised in a Christian home, my daughter, came home that day and shared this news with her father and me, to which we had to privately schedule an appointment with her teacher and ask where she got that fact. She explained that was something she had always heard. We asked that before she educated our child on something she'd heard that she may want to verify. We explained to her, as any public search would show, that, Chi (or X) is the first letter in the Greek word for Christ. In the early days of the Christian church, Christians used the letter X as a secret symbol to indicate their membership in the church to others. If you know the Greek meaning of X, Xmas and Christmas essentially mean the same thing: Christ + mas = Christmas. She was astonished at this information and apologetic as well. She influenced our daughter through her innocence of knowledge and we, in turn, influenced her through our education and facts.

Another similar situation comes to mind, although not involving a child or children, it does affect innocence or ignorance. A new Christian friend of mine and I were having lunch at her apartment one day, and I noticed a photo of her and a gentleman. She told me that the man was her brother, who had recently passed away. She said he was outstanding in making things out of wood. As our time together progressed, she told me of her excitement in becoming a Christian and living a godly life. She had thus far enjoyed all the people she had met and was learning much about the Bible and Christianity itself. She continued to tell me how her brother had made her a wooden peace sign, but to be a good Christian and walk a godly life she threw it away. Perplexed I asked why she would do such a thing? She informed me that a fellow Christian woman had told her the symbol was sacrilegious, as it represented the cross broken and upside down. My heart was crushed. This woman has trashed the last tangible memory she had of her now dead brother due to an ignorance of information given by another party. I apologized to my friend and explained that the other person, though misinformed meant well, she should always research things herself before making such rash adjustments in her life, especially ones this impactful.

According to the "Encyclopedia Britannica", Holtom, a pacifist, Christian man and gifted artist in the 1950s, in Britain during the anti-war movement, determined a distinct symbol should be created to bring awareness to their anti-war cause and successfully established the Campaign for Nuclear Disarmament (CND). Initially, he wanted the Christian cross in the center of the circle. However, this met opposition from members of the anti-war movement, as well as controversy from the church. These opponents felt the peace sign meaning of the cross might be confused with a Christian cause when in fact, the purpose was to cease nuclear arms. Frustrated and in deep misery and despair, Holtom began to draw himself in this state of anguish. He envisioned himself helpless and defeated. What resulted was a peace sign meaning with two parts: One part illustrating human stick figure hanging upside down, symbolizing helplessness. The second part was depicting arms outstretched symbolizing complete surrender. This design, if carefully observed, also contains the letters N and D, which stand for Nuclear Disarmament. Holtom made 500 copies of the peace sign and distributed the symbol on lollipop wrappers and flyers for the anti-war cause. This impressive distribution of the peace symbol and its corresponding anti-war symbol went viral, and the Campaign for Nuclear Disarmament adopted Holtom's symbol as the official peace icon for their cause. Later, the peace sign meaning gained influence in the United States as a symbol for peace instead of war. During the late 1960s-70s, Holtom's peace symbol was reproduced and mass distributed as an icon protesting the Vietnam War. It still stands strong as an easily recognizable icon representing harmony, union and the idea that love, not war is an ideal concept for the world.

Again, my friend, although she no longer had her brother or the wooden symbol he made for her, was amazed and appreciative at this information. That knowledge now would allow her to influence others through education and facts.

Innocence is one thing, ignorance another. Both can influence people in which we come in contact. Children, I believe, are exceptionally alert to people, personalities and character traits. At only three years old I knew my step-father was not a nice person (to put it mildly). If you've read my book *God, are You listening?* you know all the details. Most children can meet someone and know instantly if they like them merely by the way they present themselves or the energy they emit. Trust the children in your lives. Listen to them. As a teacher, I can tell you it is true that when one teaches, two learn.

chapter eighteen

The Impact of Everyday Living

As I have shared some moments that have influenced and impacted my life throughout this book, I am confident a few special people have crossed your thoughts as well. Whether good influences or bad, music or ministers, parents or people you meet for a mere moment, everyone is influencing someone at any given point. We are born a blank slate. Through the course of time, we are influenced by the stimuli in which we come in contact. These influence us and leave impressions on us that we carry on throughout our lives and even infiltrate to others.

I encourage you to be aware of the legacy you are leaving. People will remember it at your funeral. If it's a bad memory they may not bring it up but trust me, it WILL be remembered. As H. Jackson Brown said, *"People may not remember exactly what you did, or what you said, but they will never forget how you made them feel."* We encounter people every minute of the day. From the moment we are born we are being formed and influenced by others, raised to a certain standard and belief and ultimately becoming a unique and quality individual.

I can only speak as a business owner, woman, and mother. Yes, we know motherhood provides some of our greatest joys but also some of our greatest tests. As mothers, we need to make a conscious effort to realize that our children are gifts to us from God and we are merely their caretakers. Yes, we WILL make mistakes. That's a fact! Having children of my own, I have called my mother and apologized to her for whatever I might have put her through during my childhood years. But I have also called to thank her for the influences, the wisdom, the times I thought she was ruining my life but was genuinely loving me.

Dozens of mothers say they wish they could do it again correctly or change something, many things. Many parents feel they've done everything right and still had it blow up in their faces with the outcome of their children. We only have a short time to impact and influence our kids' lives (positively or negatively) by our actions and reactions to those around us. Our children were God's children before they were ours. Unbelievably, He loves them more than we do. He knew them before they were in our womb (Jer. 1:5). Hannah knew this best, and although barren she prayed for a child. "For this child I prayed, and the Lord granted my petition." (1 Sam 1:27). Perhaps there are some of you who were also told you could not have children, prayed, and now have a miracle terrorizing your house and mesmerizing your heart at the same time. I am one of those people.

My mother has eight children, of which, as you know, I am the oldest. We are all happy, healthy, attractive, serving the Lord people. How did she do it? Having my own children, I asked her once. She said she gave her children to the Lord. Dedicating means we will not only depend on the Lord to help us bring them up but that we will accept our children as they were created. As I mentioned before, my daughter was born a strong-willed child. She came out kicking, screaming and demanding her rights be known. She was one of those children who truly enjoyed time-out because it meant she was getting special attention that no one else was getting. She is an overachiever. All great traits especially for a woman in a man's world, not so great for a mother dealing with a three-year-old or a teenager. However, these are the traits that were instilled in her before I knew she would be born, traits that make her an amazing mother and compassionate nurse. I truly believe that these traits in her will be used to change the world someday. Who would I be as a parent to quench that spirit in her to make my life easier for today? I have had to learn how to accept her as she is and still demand the respect due to as a parent. Looking at the woman she has become, I believe it was a long but successful road.

As women, we do a lot. We are responsible for teaching our children, nurturing our marriage, ministering to others, perhaps attending Bible studies and church activities, etc. Maybe you even handle the family finances, meal planning, are a friendly neighbor or take care of an aging parent. Your pace of living is probably like most, hectic and stressful at times with kids, school, job, other obligations, and perhaps you try to squeeze in some personal goals (mine is losing weight- where does that even fit in?) I always have a running list of things to do. Check off a few, add a few more.

Our lives can become "busy" and ultimately become enemy of our souls. (Being Under Satan's Yoke). Add stresses like teenage rebellion, marriage problems, finances, illness, etc. and it makes one wonder "Where is this abundant life we hear about?" Unfortunately, the intent is to cripple us when we are most vulnerable, to make us feel we don't measure up, that we are no good. A favorite tactics is to try to distract us from our destiny, our plan and purpose for our lives by putting negativities in our paths, tempting us to compare ourselves, our lives and our circumstances with others and keeping us too busy to be what we were set out to be. That's why it is so important for us to know what our destiny has set for US to do.

Joyce Meyer always talks about how she wanted to be a worship leader, and she was convinced that is what God wanted her to do. So, she set out to do what she felt was her calling and become a worship leader, but she was not getting anywhere and was not being blessed. Eventually, she realized that she was meant to minister, just not through song. She was called to preach, and we now see how God has blessed her through that anointing.

We all have unique gifts, but few women view themselves as gifted. Maybe that's not surprising, given the way society defines gifted. We express gifted as brilliant, elite, beautiful, the privileged, the few who are tapped into a unique gene pool or club. This leaves the everyday people feeling inadequate.

But fortunately, there is good news. If you are familiar with the Bible you know that God uses cracked pots. There are countless examples in there but here are a few of my favorites. Noah was a drunk (Gen, 9:20-24) yet his purpose was to build the ark, Abraham was too old (Gen. 17:17) but he became the Father of all nations, Jacob was a liar (Gen 27:19) but was the Father of 12 tribes or Israel, Leah was ugly (Gen. 29:17) yet she gave birth to Jacob's 12 sons. Joseph was abused and banished by his siblings (Gen 37:23) yet became the Prince of Egypt, Davis had an affair and was a murderer ((2 Sam. 11:1-24) and became a great king and hailed as a man after God's own heart. Heck, Lazarus was dead (John 11:14) and yet he was raised three times from death.

We all have a unique and special plan and purpose for our life. It may merely be to sow into your child, to raise him or her to be a kind, loving, self-sufficient man or woman and send them out to shine their light among the world through their actions, words and deeds. You should know that whatever the plan is for us as individuals no one else can fulfill it. Like the cracked pots of the Bible, the Lord didn't find someone else to take those people's places. In fact, I suspect they said, "No, send someone else." But the Lord had a purpose that only THEY could fulfill. You have all that you need to fulfill your purpose. Absolutely nothing is lacking in you. The enemy wants to hinder your journey of fulfilling your destiny by distracting you with fear, doubt, unbelief and unnecessary busyness.

In 1997, I had a hysterectomy and was petrified. Mostly because I was afraid the doctors were going to give me enough anesthesia for my body weight. I am a lightweight when it comes to any kind of drugs. It takes very little of anything to do a lot to me. But my doctor was adamant about me not waking up mid-surgery and insisted that the appropriate dose would be administered. The day of my surgery I was all prayed up, had written letters to my children in case I did not come out of operation alive. And just in case the doctor, who assured me he had done hundreds of these, had forgotten who he was dealing, with I written on the bottom of my feet (on one foot) *two kids* (on the other) *need me*. There was no way I was going to let this doctor think of me as just another routine hysterectomy surgery. All said and done, it took me quite a while to come out of the anesthesia due to everything I had endured, but when I finally lifted my groggy eyelids and woke up, my nurse was opening the blinds in my room. As the sun peered through the cracks in the mini blinds, I thought to myself "I'm alive!" The nurse upon my awakening told me I'd missed all the excitement and proceeded to tell me of Princess Diana's death. Princess Diana and I shared the same birthday and were the same age. Although I was saddened by the death of such a lovely person, I rejoiced inside at the fact that I was alive and looking at the sun shining through the window, able to leave a legacy for my children after all.

The masterpiece, the legacy, we are molding is partly determined by the choices we make at any given moment. Your legacy can only be accomplished moment by moment. Someone has influenced all of us in our lives. Whether negative or positive words spoken by parents, teachers, peers, and even strangers begin to form a picture in our hearts of who we are, who we may become. Sometimes messages are derived from the absence of words and warmth. By the time we reach our teenage years, experts tell us each of us already has formed most of our beliefs about ourselves. By then our interpretation of the message around us has helped us decide whether we measure up and our personal identity is generally, in place. I want you to understand the impact you have on those around you just by being. You are you. There is no one else like you. NO one else can make the difference in the world you impact that you can. Remember, your playing small does not serve the world.

Choose to bring light and love. Choose to leave a positive legacy. Your speech can bless your children, your actions can strengthen your marriage, your prayers will move mountains in your lives, and your character will influence others. Don't worry if it doesn't happen overnight. We are all works in progress. Did you know you can still be a masterpiece AND be a work in progress? It's true. You are wonderfully made, and there is no one else like you. I encourage you to continue to press forward with passion, pursuing the depths of who you were created to be. Realize the work God is doing in you is an ongoing, evolving process of growth toward maturity. Release the frustrations you may have about yourself and the fact that you don't have your act together. What matters is that you leave where you are today and move on to the next step. Continue to develop and define and refine your life and character and the legacy you wish to leave behind.

You CAN influence your legacy and purpose, either for good or bad. No one else has the power to keep you from fulfilling your destiny. It does not matter what others may say about you or what they have done. None of that can prevent you from fulfilling your destiny and leaving the legacy you desire. I challenge you to love the way you want to be loved. Gandhi said it best when he said, *"Be the change that you want to see in the world."* You cannot harvest something you do not plant. Start today by making choices that will contribute to a future worth having. And remember, your children are watching your every move, and you are, by your actions and reactions impacting their lives.

Serve others unselfishly. Give and expect nothing in return. Your children will see this trait. Be an example. My stepfather used to flip a bird at any car that passed him on the street. I once knew a guy who cussed at a car in the parking lot AT CHURCH for cutting out in front of us as we were leaving after service. Both these situations and these people had an impact on my life and me - but negatively. So how do you respond to someone having a bad day? Do you respond or react? Make choices that count. Monitor your motives. Focus on being, not doing!

There is a vision for your life. Every day. Look for the blessings. Buy a blessing book, and every day find at least three things in which you are grateful. Some days will be more difficult than others, but soon you will start noticing even the smallest things. Write out your plans for your children. Pray for them. Pray for their spouses. Take time in your busyness to rest. Look at it as an investment in the legacy you are leaving. Rest your souls not just your mind, body, and eyes.

You carry one of the greatest gifts to change lives, the power to be a blessing. (from page 91 -*God, are You listening?*) *What are we teaching our children? The generation that will take care of us when we are old and incapacitated? That will run our country?*

Have we taught them the golden rule: Do unto others as you would have others do unto you? It's such a simple rule. Unfortunately, it's almost become a cliché. What example have we set for our children to follow? I try to instill this in my children no matter the age or circumstance they are in. Someone is a bully, someone is rude, he broke my heart, she's being bossy - whatever the scenario, the answer is simple. We often judge others by their actions but want to be judged by our intentions. We want mercy for us but judgment for them. What if we stop casting the first stone and just start loving and giving to others? I want more for my kids.

What examples have we set for them to follow? Like I said earlier, we often want mercy for ourselves and judgment for others. Our hearts were created to love. We, as women, are tender, emotional nurturers. (from page 93- *God, are You listening?*) *"I challenge you when sitting at a stoplight, pray; when waiting for your child in front of the schoolyard or slowing down at a school crossing, claim that school for Christ, even if you don't have children who attend there; when standing in the grocery store pay for the person in front of you. Make a game out of it if you must and see how many times a day you can pray. Then try to beat your record the next day. It doesn't take much, and it will make a difference. The enemy wants us to be too busy to pray.... too busy to notice, let alone care.* If you feel overwhelmed, guess what? You may find comfort in knowing that Jesus did too. Mark 6:31 tells us that Jesus mentions he needs to go away and rest for a while. Taking a break is NOT a waste of time, it is a time of refueling. My mother used to lie eight pillows in a row on the floor every afternoon and make us lie down for 20 minutes while she would sit in a chair and read or paint or just sit back with her eyes closed. I suppose that was her daily refueling time.

So, pass the torch of power, of being a blessing to the next generation by leaving a legacy worthy of noting. Make a grand impact to even the lowliest. Believe it or not, there is a high purpose and calling placed on your life. This calling is activated the minute you are born. We are born blank slates and the stimuli we experience throughout our lives leaves an impression that we carry with us even into future generations. The legacy will be there no matter what you do, say or believe as well as what you don't do, say or believe. Choose to leave a legacy that makes a positive difference in the lives of your children and others you meet along the road of life throughout your 1440 minutes in a day. And live your life with wonder, purpose and positive influence.

ABOUT
THE AUTHOR

Michelle Bryant is multi-faceted. Growing up the oldest of eight children, she was destined to be a leader, mentor, and motivator. As an entrepreneur, inspirational speaker, and author of six books, she has shared her story, passion, and light. Whether it is through boys and girls in a residential treatment facility suffering from issues such as abuse and neglect, syndicated radio shows, or live in front of women's groups, Michelle's message encourages and gives the audience hope. She is a radiant example of an overcomer who truly forgives and thrives. She speaks from her heart delivering an encouraging, transparent message of hope, healing, victory and empowerment.

You can check out her works at: www.divinelyfocused.com

Made in the USA
Columbia, SC
15 August 2022

64602750R00062